THE DEAD GOOD
BOOK OF

NAMINGS
~AND~
BABY WELCOMING
CEREMONIES

Edited by
Jonathan How
with Sue Gill and John Fox

Engineers of the Imagination
Ulverston, Cumbria, England

© Engineers of the Imagination 1999
First published by
Engineers of the Imagination, 1999

ISBN 0 9527159 2 9 Paperback

Publisher
Engineers of the Imagination
Welfare State International
Lanternhouse, The Ellers
Ulverston, Cumbria
LA12 0AA
01229 581127

Distribution
Edge of Time Ltd
BCM Edge
London WC1N 3XX
07000 780536

Printing (contents)
Greenwood Recycled Printing
Lakeside
off Warehouse Hill
Marsden, Huddersfield
HD7 6AE
01484 844841

Printing (cover)
Buckingham Colour Press
Riverside Works
Bridge Street, Buckingham
MK18 1EN
01280 824000

**Typesetting, Design
and Layout**
Jonathan How
BCM Visions
London WC1N 3XX
0870 444 2566

SUPPORTED BY
THE NATIONAL LOTTERY
THROUGH
THE ARTS COUNCIL
OF ENGLAND

northern
arts

Engineers of the Imagination is the publishing arm of

Galactic Smallholdings Ltd
Registered Charity N° 265461

To Daniel, Hannah, Billy, Francesca, George, Isabel, Jack, Kylie, Nik, Richard and Thom – all the Welfare State International children (1968-1998) who unwittingly allowed their proud parents to try out a naming ceremony on them

ACKNOWLEDGEMENTS

In October 1997, 10 people (Gilly Adams, Sue Gill, Roger Bloomfield, Jonathan How, Chris Coates, Hilary Hughes, Hannah Fox, Tanya Peixoto, John Fox and Dot Queen) from Welfare State International went for a week's retreat to Fawcett Mill in North Cumbria. The aim was to collectively write this book ... in a week. We came up with the structure and the list of contents, wrote about 15% on site, enjoyed good food and a couple of walks, but instead of knuckling down to it, we got excited about a marketing plan to produce the next six Dead Good Guides. This took avoidance tactics to the level of an artform!

In addition to those mentioned above we'd like to thank: Jenny Dell, Professor Ron Grimes, Maggie and Boris Howarth, Lois Lambert, Pete Moser, Christine and Malcolm Mahony, Catriona Stamp, Ann West and Lucy MacKeith. We are also grateful to the Arts Council of England and Northern Arts for their support.

"Travelbag" and "Heartsong" (from *Life by Drowning*, Bloodaxe Books) are reproduced by kind permission of Jeni Couzyn. Permissions for other reproductions of text have been sought.

Front cover: naming ceremony of Ewan Mahony. Back cover: relief plaque made by David Haley to announce the birth of Claudia Haley. Papercuts throughout are by Martin Brockman and cartoons by John Fox.

CONTENTS GUIDE

TO A CHILD BEFORE BIRTH

This summer is your perfect summer. Never will the skies
So stretched and strident be with blue
As these you do not see; never will the birds surprise
With such light flukes the ferns and fences
As these you do not hear. This year the may
Smells like rum-butter, and day by day
The petals slip from the cups like lover's hands,
Tender and tired and satisfied. This year the haws
Will form as your fingers form, and when in August
The Sun first stings your eyes,
The fruit will be red as brick and free to the throstles.
Oh but next year the may
Will have its old smell of plague about it; next year
The songs of the birds be selfish,
     the skies have rain;
Next year the apples will be tart
     again.
But do not always grieve
For the unseen summer. Perfection
     is not the land you leave,
it is the pole you measure from; it
     gives
Geography to your ways and
     wanderings.
What is your perfection is another's
     pain;
And because she in impossible
     season loves
So in her blood for you the bright
     bird sings.

Norman Nicholson

The case for ceremonies in the everyday of people's lives

Welfare State International Engineers of the Imagination

Founded in 1968 by John Fox and Sue Gill, Welfare State International is an arts company now based in Ulverston, Cumbria. After gaining a world-wide reputation for creating celebratory events with communities and for pioneering prototypes of site specific events such as lantern festivals, carnival bands and fireshows, the company has turned its attention to vernacular art. "We are seeking a culture which may be less materially based but where more people will actively participate and gain the power to celebrate moments that are wonderful and significant. This may be building our own houses, naming our children, burying our dead, announcing partnerships, marking anniversaries, creating new spaces for secular ceremonies and producing whatever drama, stories, songs, rituals, ceremonies, pageants and jokes that are relevant to new values and new iconography." This work is documented in **Engineers of the Imagination** (Methuen 1983, 1990).

Many people believe that today we live in troubled times. We always have. The trouble is that the trouble varies with the scale and purpose of the ditch, the bullet, the spade or the rescue remedy. We are persuaded that it's worse than ever. The story goes that we live in a post-religious age where our community or society has gone, isolating us in a violent and polluted environment with at least a rampant axeman and a rising sea level outside. True or not, media gossip reinforces our insecurity.

Most escape remedies such as religion, alcohol, CDs or birdwatching are a pleasurable mix of vision and illusion. Ceremonies and rituals are no different. They can be equally addictive, sentimental and nostalgic reinforcements of outmoded tradition or they can be:

- Life enhancing celebrations of our shared humanity.

- A magnet to draw families together in community.

- A rope bridge over the dizzy void.

- A memory bank of mutual experience.

The need to seek new patterns for contemporary ritual came to us after extensive experience as theatre directors of site-specific events involving thousands of participants in fireshows, carnivals and lantern festivals.

Concurrently we had witnessed ceremonies for funerals, weddings and baptisms which were ugly, unconnected with the participants, propagandist, often expensive and frequently exploitative.

At critical cross-roads where we need all the support we can get, or moments when we need a unique celebration, when we need to shout and share our being with a wide congregation there is, certainly in England, a dearth of good ceremonial practice.

We have applied our theatrical expertise, knowledge of aesthetics, drama, music and stage management, for instance, to these particular occasions.

We began with Death. Our book on funerals, the first of the *Dead Good Guides*, demonstrates how much control and choice we have over funeral rites once we free ourselves from taboos and outmoded traditions. Many people have written to us since to confirm that facing their own deaths and designing a funeral in consultation with friends and family is far from morbid, but stimulates creativity and even awakens reasons for living.

Retirement, leaving home, stopping work (either through choice or redundancy), changing jobs, changing status, reaching a birthday decade, moving or building a house, divorcing, as well as in the traditional areas of birth, christening, coming of age, marrying or dying; we could all benefit from considered declarations of our position with a sympathetic group. The question for a fragmented society is not whether we need rites of passage ceremonies but rather what form should they take and who should provide them? Should there be training for new groups of specialist celebrants or should people learn to do it for themselves perhaps, even at school?

The experience of writing our manual on funerals and learning from participants on the many subsequent courses has been most humbling. Once we stopped assuming that religion had to be the stuff of deities and pieties, institutions and retributions and realised there is a common need to reclaim a sense of the sacred, to inform secular rites, we came to understand that many of our neighbours have their own "religious" sense of the inexplicable.

People experience great wonders. Not just when their children are born and when they fall in love. Not just when faced with strange coincidences and before "Awesome Nature", but also in everyday surprises and communication with friends.

For many of us, the daily grind, ambition, our careers, the news, the welter of the trivial, obscures the central focus. But once removed from this clutter, many of us have a sense of the miraculous in the mundane. Even, or perhaps especially, in troubled times.

INTRODUCTION

How this book works

This book is divided into five parts. If your interest is of an armchair nature you will probably gravitate more towards the sections at the front of the book. If, on the other hand, you're contemplating carrying out a naming ceremony yourself then the best place to start is about halfway through.

Part One
looks at the anthropological and philosophical ideas around conception, birth and naming. What other people get up to in their cultures can give us inspiration for improving our own.

Part Two
investigates traditions around birth and naming as they are practised in Britain today. If you want to do something different then first of all be sure that you understand the thing that you want to be different from.

Part Three
tells you what you have to do, legally, when you have a new baby. It will also help you with the business of actually choosing a name.

Part Four
looks at ways in which you can improve the circumstances which surround the birth of a new baby. In this section we move on to naming ceremonies and hear about a number of examples.

Part Five
is for those who have decided to go ahead and organise their own ceremony. It's a nuts and bolts manual which covers everything from celebrants to ceremonial space and poetry to papercuts.

What is a Naming Ceremony?

A marking, usually public, an affirmation, a declaration, a witnessing, a demonstrating at a particular moment, usually celebratory, in which some person or thing is given a name by some person or persons. In a rite of passage the recipient moves through a symbolic gateway from one state to another and the rest of our friends acknowledge this changed presence within their tribe.

There can be a sense of travelling from generalised "non being" to an identity. Namings reflect the value (good or bad) we place on that named. To be named at all, like a tropical storm, is a measure of some importance, and the name is usually written down.

Both name and ceremony may be simple or complex, short or long, linked with hopes and blessings, accounts of the past and dreams of the future and any aesthetic facilitation or elaboration via temporary or permanent architecture, performance, poetry, music, food etc as appropriate. Symbols and stories (conscious or unconscious) that are part of the (stated or unstated) shared value structure of those involved may well be incorporated.

"I name this galleon "Good Fellow" and may all Pilgrims who sail in her be for ever prosperous and smiling".

"We call our daughter Spicy Pankhurst Amethyst Montgomery. Or SPAM for short."

Mass Media Comment and Public Attitudes

Media interest in secular naming ceremonies is currently growing. Publications ranging from popular magazine *Bella* to *The Sunday Times* plus Talk Radio and The Archers are featuring baby namings, even endorsed by the 1998 Labour Party Conference.

Taking Christianity out of a christening is the gist of the headlines, but the political agenda is a rescue bid for "the family" in its traditional definition. Strengthening family ties, underlining the father's responsibilities, in particular, by way of guidance from registrars is being proposed as a substitute, in this increasingly secular age, for the role previously taken by the church.

"Many people who are not particularly religious feel that birth, marriage and death should be marked 'properly' in Church or synagogue. Others – both the religious and the devoutly sceptical – think such an approach is a little hypocritical.

What is certain is that we all share a deep human need to celebrate the great events in every life with due solemnity.

That is why it is perhaps inevitable that the Government is considering allowing registrars to conduct 'alternative baptisms', complete with sponsors instead of god parents, and wise words from the registrar instead of the vicar."

Editorial, Daily Mail 25/5/98

The Rt Hon Ann Widdecombe, MP, Shadow Health Secretary and former Home Office Minister says:

"The ceremony is a load of rubbish for the very simple reason that there is no need for it. I'm sick of this business, people want it all ways, they reject the Church but they want the equivalent Ceremony. Well, forget it – it's totally namby-pamby. Frankly, if you bring it into the realms of the registry office, it's a waste of time and effort."

The Independent, September 1998

Supporting Families

was a paper, published in November 1998, by the Ministerial Group on the Family. This working party was set up by the Prime Minister to develop a coherent Government strategy to increase the support and help available to families. Over 6,000 copies of the full document were sent to relevant bodies as well as professionals and individuals. Over 3,000 people accessed Supporting Families on the Home Office website. Over 1,000 responses to the consultation were received. Section 4.17 suggested the promotion of baby-naming ceremonies and enlarging the role of registrars to enable them to conduct such ceremonies. The stated aim being "to help parents make a public, long-term commitment to their children and bring together friends and the wider family". Of the 158 responses to this proposal, 111 people were in agreement that there is a need for these ceremonies and were supportive of the proposals: 43 responses opposed the idea of baby-naming ceremonies and questioned the need for secular ceremonies. Some of the responses did not oppose the idea of baby-naming ceremonies, but questioned whether registrars would be the best people to perform them. One response foresaw problems with conflicting demands for the use of venues for marriages and baby-naming ceremonies. There were also practical questions: for example, when and where would the ceremonies take place? If there is a demand, the most popular times will be at the weekends or evenings. Often the only suitable room is the "Marriage Room". There were other questions of a technical nature concerning the status of these events, whether they would be recorded and, if they were, what their legal relationship would be to the original registration entry. The conclusion was that there is a demand for a service which register offices are at present unable to fulfil due to statutory limitations imposed on their functions.

How Artists got involved with Naming Ceremonies

Artists with Welfare State International, the celebratory arts company, began creating their own ceremonies in

1969. They began with namings, as their own children were born, and moved on to applying similar skills to help friends and colleagues who wanted to arrange their own weddings. Latterly, they have been involved in funerals and memorial services. Approximately thirty naming ceremonies have been held, mostly in the UK, but some in the USA and others in the Australian outback! The elements – earth, air, fire and water – have always been a starting point. Thus, a gathering in the chilly Yorkshire landscape might involve the outdoor firing of a kiln containing clay birds or animals, to be given to the children as mementos of the day. In Australia, decorated parasols to keep the sun off and a feast of mangoes would be more appropriate.

Each ceremony is distinctive – to respect the personal wishes and feelings of the families involved and to work with the local materials, climate and culture.

Children have been named on a beach, in a cave with an underground waterfall, in the garden, on the open moor, in the living room, on a college campus and in woodland. Different times of day, from dawn to dusk – whatever felt right – and all seasons of the year.

These ceremonies have included story telling of creation myths, sometimes through the use of shadow theatre, music, specially written songs and words, food, gifts, surprises and sometimes a gathering of people taking a short journey together through the landscape for different stages of the ceremony.

Training in visual and performing arts means that artists have experience to call on when planning and preparing a ceremony. They know about words, music, design and layout of the space for the ceremony to take place in, preparation and rigging spaces in advance, thinking about how to do it and how long it takes. People with a performance presence can be good to lead a ceremony – as they will not be overcome by nerves. They can help create the right atmosphere with their sense of space and timing, stillness and focus.

The Naming of Dan Fox

A Chinese New Year story seemed a good starting-point. It told of a poor man who lived outside a city and earned his living through selling fireworks. At New Year, unlike his neighbours who spent their money on food, he bought a statue of a beautiful girl. He took it home and honoured it with food. In time it came to life, and she began to prepare his food and care for him. They lived together and had a child. But an inescapable longing overcame her to return to her former state, and he was left with the child who in her turn honoured the statue with flowers ... We decided to make the story into a simple mime play, with a narrator, and specially composed music and songs ... As the performance was planned for outside, the actors and musicians rehearsed and played music all over the dale – particularly in the chosen spot, a sheltered clearing dotted with foxgloves, bracken, wild roses and butterflies. Everything depended on the weather, and the day was perfect. About 60 people arrived, including several other babies to be included in the ceremony. We sat on a grassy slope and waited. Fire-crackers went off on the hill facing us and singing was heard from the wood on our left as the band approached. The poor man, in oatmeal robe, white wooden mask and enormous canvas shoes, appeared near the straw bales (indicating his house) and the slow dreamlike play began. The movement was closer to dance, gestures were kept to an absolute minimum and frozen in the pauses; they looked like life-sized puppets. It took over 20 or 30 minutes, during which time the score of children who were watching were enchanted.

At the end of the play, as the father held his child triumphantly, priceless Japanese fireworks were again released on the opposite hill ... The poor man began the procession to the top of the hill, and we followed with the musicians. A bonfire blazed, a red banner flapped and coloured smoke billowed up – this was to be the naming. At the sound of a gong the first parent went forward, held aloft his tiny son and shouted his name into the wind."

Northern Echo July 1969

Naming Ceremonies for Buildings, Boats and Organisations

Sometimes situations other than a child or person require a naming ceremony. Houses, boats, organisations, groups or buildings may all at some point become named. Often the acquisition of a name is the cherry on the cake. Much work has gone before, in order to get to the point of giving it a name.

A new house for example. This may have been a building project for many months, or the ordeal of searching for a house, buying, packing and moving. In these instances the naming ceremony can be the confirmation of the change that has taken place and a commitment to the next phase of living.

When might you have a naming ceremony for a house?

If it is a new house to you there are several clear points when a ceremony might be appropriate. Laying the foundations, raising the roof, getting the keys, moving in, house-warming party, first anniversary of living there ...

What might you do?

If it is as early as laying the foundations, you may wish to bury or inscribe something here – it could be an object never to be found again, or it could be a slate slab at the front step with the name carved in bold letters. You may have a gathering of builders, family neighbours to witness the slab being laid. Perhaps a toast.

If your naming is later, maybe a house warming party is a good moment. A group of friends together, maybe children. Perhaps a treasure hunt to look for the plaque – when it is found the ceremonial screwing into place on the door or the gate can happen. A nice moment later is when you can announce your new home with change of address cards, and proudly include the new house name in the address.

Boats seem to usually have names. Boats also have launches, and these two ceremonies are often interwoven. Smashing the bottle is extravagant and exciting. Ceremonially it works well because it is good theatre, providing a build-up of tension, the climax (ie the moment of naming), and the festivities afterwards. Other naming ways may be to make the first trip with a name flag flying high or to hold a party on the vessel and invite the local sign-writer to come and paint on the same day.

Buildings that are municipal often have opening ceremonies. A person is appointed to lead the event, which can culminate in another piece of good theatre, the revealing of a name that is hidden or secret. Perhaps a new wing is being named. The cutting of a ribbon and entering the new space creates a ceremonial transition. You may choose a significant person with a connection to the name to be the ribbon-cutter. Inside could be a big name cake – a great way to share and spread the news of the new name.

Groups or organisations are less tangible things to name. A band, for example, can go through many name attempts, but it is often the playing of the first public gig that confirms or stamps this choice of name.

If you wish to have a naming ceremony for an organisation, it may be a good idea to try and find something that exists already that you can build the ceremony around. Do you have a logo, or headed notepaper? Perhaps you create a recognisable artefact or are associated with a clear image. A new bird watching club, for example, has excellent ornithological imagery to draw upon. The creation of a poster or flyer with your chosen image on can announce your name, but perhaps later, at your first group outing you could make biscuits in your special shape, eat them, laugh and name yourselves!

The choice of name for groups or organisations can often prove tricky. Too many good suggestions ... and you may find that the selection process – a vote or the picking out of a hat – is actually a naming ceremony in action. All the quantities are present. The tension, the expectation, the selection, and moment of declaration! Moments like this can often be charged with emotion and opinion. Now is the time to try and celebrate the choice. Even a simple drink or informal chat about the new identity can get the name warmed up and welcome in its new home.

Hannah Fox

INFANT JOY

"I have no name:

"I am but two days old."

What shall I call thee?

"I happy am,

"Joy is my name."

Sweet joy befall thee!

Pretty joy!

Sweet joy but two days old,

Sweet joy I call thee:

Thou dost smile,

I sing the while,

Sweet joy befall thee!

William Blake, 1789

PART ONE
SOME RUMINATIONS
ON NAMES AND
NAMING CEREMONIES

If you're the type of parent that doesn't want your child to be christened just "because it's the done thing" then you'll probably also want to get a broader perspective on the business of both naming and ceremonies. Here are John Fox's views:

What's in a Name?

Although "Infant Joy" (opposite) and my own "You won't know" (see next page) are two hundred years apart, both poems express the euphoria commonly felt at birth. The second poem with its tests, telephones and statistics is of our time of surplus but in each case the joy in a new being is unbounded and unquestioned.

from **People of the Lake** by Richard LEAKEY and Roger LEWIN, Collins, London 1979

Why have a baby?

Not all new babies are welcome. In *People of the Lake*, the palaeontologist Richard Leakey describes a gathering and hunting community in South America in 1960.

"When the baby – a boy – arrived, Bahimi (his mother) promptly killed him, explaining tearfully that he would have taken milk away from her other infant Ariwari, who was still nursing at the age of almost three. Rather than risk Ariwari not surviving the trauma and hazard of early weaning, Bahimi killed her new born son. Sad but necessary."

Leakey doesn't report if he was given a name before or after his death.

You won't know

You won't know,
Charles Jasper,
(or whoever you come to be
called).
You won't know
Until you read this later,
just how many warm tears
welled deep at your birth.

Around the nation
sighs and lovely cryings,
so happy at your
BEING.

Against the odds.
Against the tests.
Against the shaking heads,
which murmured
NO
so many times.

YOU ARE HERE AND WELL.

You won't know,
but,
You have a weight, .
a name
and already your own surprise.

SIX POUNDS TEN OUNCES.

"Six pounds ten ounces"
has been scribbled by us all,
from breathy telephone,
and excited neighbours knocking
on the door.

Your name we share,
But then
you won't know,
That,
You've got black and CURLY hair!

Hello and welcome
To Nick and Gill's
SON.

John Fox, 1991

In the UK, away from such Darwinian pressures, the state would prosecute any mother who killed her baby (even if the infant was severely brain damaged). Our value system of "life at all costs" and the great significance of "Baby" is fundamental. As any rite of passage reflects and reinforces an underlying value system, the system should be clear and agreed by individuals in society. This is not always the case, particularly before a millennium when new and old ideas tend to clash.

For example, Britain has the highest teenage pregnancy rate in Europe and the highest number of single mothers, yet our baby naming and welcoming ceremonies such as they are, whether religious or secular, presume two involved parents of different sexes in a traditional family structure. It could be that we need to invent new ceremonies to mark the separate needs of mother and father, as well as the infant; ceremonies to change name as we now move nomadically from one family to another, and dignified ceremonies to mark the birth of a baby who will be adopted or fostered.

Perhaps it is asking too much for the name of the baby and the naming ceremony itself to reflect the motivation and intention of breeding but in a society where babies and children are sometimes treated as living dolls, where we pass on female roles through Sindy, Spice and drum majorettes, and boys' roles through toy guns and war games, the creation of babies does merit thought. At least such questions are appropriate to ask before making presumptions that all births should be celebrated or celebrated in identical ways.

When is a baby made?

Other cultures are more aware of and celebrate the moment of conception. If we focussed on this rather than on birth or subsequent naming or the romance and sentiment of it all, there could be less unwanted pregnancies.

In *Journey to the Crocodile's Nest*, a monograph to accompany a film recording the burial of a young child who died at a small Aboriginal settlement in the Northern Territory of Australia, its author Howard Morphy writes about one spiritual cycle.

Ancestral beings left behind reservoirs of spiritual power in the countryside. These places, usually those associated with a major creative act of the Ancestral being concerned, can contain conception spirits, which are thought to be effective in the conception of children.

Belief in conception spirits does not necessarily involve a denial of the role of sexual intercourse in reproduction, but concerns a complementary creative force which operates in conjunction with biological processes. For the Yolngu the conception spirit is usually identified through association with an unusual event that happens at the time the child first moves in its mother's womb. The father may, for example, encounter a rough patch of water when out at sea in his canoe, near a place created by one of his clan's Ancestral beings. Later he may dream of the Ancestral being and take this as a sign that a conception spirit associated with that Ancestor at the place concerned entered his wife and caused the child to grow. The child will receive a name that connects it with the Ancestral being and it is this relationship that provides a person with his or her most direct spiritual connection with the clan's Ancestral beings.

When people die their spiritual component returns to the land associated with the Ancestral beings from who it was derived. It then becomes part of the reservoir of Ancestral power, to be called upon again to act on behalf of clan members, as a conception spirit during the performance of ceremonies or in guiding the souls of dead clan members.

This puts our own values and "moment of naming" into perspective. It is also a good example of a religious framework linking spiritual and Earthly concerns in a continuum of real and symbolic time. Christianity has similar patterns including Mary's miraculous conception devoid of human intercourse, an ancestral duo of Father and Son, an ill-defined spiritual power called the Holy Ghost and an equal sense of the circle of life and death. Such symbolism can be helpful when we are overwhelmed by incomprehension.

What is a baby?

A squalling, mewling, sweet-smelling cocoon of dependency, shit, wonder and aspiration and all that, yes, but where does a baby begin and finish today? If scientists have learned to still a sperm or an egg in deep freeze, until we, or our successors, decide to bring them together, should we give each item an individual name like Wise and Morecambe, or Wait and See, or Dandy and Lion?

A Natal Address to my Child

Hail to thy puggy nose, my Darling
Fair womankind's last added scrap,
That, callow as an unfledg'd starling,
Liest screaming in the Nurse's lap.

No locks thy tender cranium boasteth,
No lashes veil thy gummy eye
And, like some steak gridiron toasteth,
Thy skin is red and crisp and dry.

Thy mouth is swollen past describing,
Its corners twisted as in scorn
Of all the Leech is now prescribing
To doctor thee, the newly born.

Sweet little lump of flannel binding,
Thou perfect cataract of clothes,
Thy many folds there's no unwinding
Small mummy without arms or toes!

And am I really then thy Mother?
My very child I cannot doubt thee,
Rememb'ring all the fuss and bother
And moans and groans I made about thee!

'Tis now thy turn to groan and grumble,
As if afraid to enter life,
To dare each whipping scar and tumble
And task and toil with which 'tis rife.

O baby of the wise round forehead,
Be not too thoughtful ere thy time;
Life is not truly quite so horrid —
Oh! how she squalls! — she can't bear rhyme!

Eliza Ogilvy, 1844

Using genetic
engineering it is conceivable that we are on the
threshold of controlling our own evolution. If
Huntington's Chorea is really genetic do we need a

ceremony when we discard the vile gene? There would be just cause for celebration.

What is an individual beyond a bunch of genes? Naming separates and each identity grows in its own way. If we do come to control our evolution, we could decide that the habit of individuation is no longer fitting. Isolation, insecurity and aggression, if they belong together, may no longer be the best way for our species to survive (if we want to survive that is). Maybe we would be better served through collective bonding with no labelling of distinctive ego at all. If we were all called Joan or Jonathan or just Jo for short, the chaos might be easier.

Anyway, what's Jo when it's grown up? Two million years ago we weren't humans. One million years ago we were. Our cultural evolution has been packed into a few thousand years in which it took longer for an ape to become man than it took for a caveman to become an Einstein. In Dawkins' book *Untangling the Rainbow*, he takes us to another end of the spectrum. Each of us is a carrier of other creatures; a metropolis of symbiotic bacteria, a flowing Humanoid Ark Royal of multifarious identities, a walking soup of genes, cells, atoms, bacteria etc.

We maintain our quaint preference for single brand names for ourselves when we are in fact whole communities. See Donovan over there. He's a planetary system. And so am I. How wonderful. Why would we kill each other? How busy celebrants we would be if we were commissioned to name each individual bacteria. And how our consciousness of self changes as new knowledge expands our perceptual horizon.

What generally happens when we name a baby?

The moment of birth is usually soon marked with congratulations, gooey commercial cards, loads of gift wrapped flowers and a few chocolatey and lacey treats. There is unseemly haste to put a name on the birth certificate. The pressure to an extent is self-invented; we have six weeks to decide, but everybody wants to know the name (and weight) of baby. Unspoken superstitions loom so that we all want to give the child that framing identity as soon as possible in case it dies and goes into limbo. Roman Catholic propaganda has babies floating in the universe for ever; never able to break into the heaven club because their abject and guilty parents failed to organise the baptism.

Some months of anxious research or pleasurable speculation have probably gone into choosing the name. Nowadays we may know its sex and health before birth, and the chances are that the mother, or the couple, and probably the grandparents too, have scoured the many lists of available names. Some name by dreaming of those heroes and heroines we aspire to. As our culture stands we don't wait to see what kind of a person the child becomes or give them the opportunity later in life to name or re-name themselves. We could change our name when we get a job or leave home, or just like the ring of the words of a new name ... We could all have stage names. But this is not yet our way.

Generally though, having to decide quickly (with too little sleep and often a new howling offspring) intellectuals might choose Blake for a boy (we did). Royalists will go for Di; young working class women will go for Ginger or another spice girl; and male football fans will settle for Ruud Huddite (you rude Geordie lad ...).

Most of the names we choose, excluding certain ethnic or religious groupings, come from clear sources. These often have a Christian or Old Testament origin (such as my own children's names Daniel and Hannah) or derive from fashionable stars, Kylie, Mel, Dylan etc. Some names, mainly surnames, still link with traditional trades such as Smith, Farmer, Driver, Baker etc (not yet Computer Analyst). Most of us are locked into these fashionable labels and never change them. But how our Gods come home.

The name we did choose or the fantasies we predicted, seemingly so suitable when our baby was a gnawsome bundle become flawed in quite a short time. Our Ruud hates football; our Ginger detests Prince Charles. Blake is *so* sixties.

Here is a case for re-naming: having a temporary name on the birth certificate and formally changing it later when Ginger is a blonde aero-engineer or Ruud is president of the Blood Bank, or like Cassius Clay, you prefer Mohammed Ali. It is in fact quite easy to change your name by Deed Poll (my wife went from Susan Fox to Sue Gill overnight), but we get attached to these quick labels and the State with its national insurance, taxation, car licensing and pensions and the finance houses with their credit ratings thrive on permanence.

What else is there in a name?

If many UK names originate with football and television obsessions, other cultures acknowledge different religions, prophets or deities. In Islam, it is Mohammed, his wives and daughters. In Catholic countries the saint on whose day the child is born. In India many of the Hindu Gods and (as Hindus believe God is manifest in everything), household objects. So a child, with a pointy nose, could be named after a carving knife. In Ghana a baby is given two names. One, the soul's name (associated with the deity of the day), given at the hour of birth, and the other, the name of a distinguished relative given by the father seven days later.

Homage, courtesy, fear, flattery, religion, fear of incest, fashion, sentiment, chance all play a part in naming. There is a fierce biological labelling in some parts of the world. In Nigeria, Aina means the delivery had complications, or Ige means delivered feet first, or Olugbodi tells us the child has an extra finger or toe.

This system would be out of order in our politically correct world of excessive surplus and institutionalised fairness where differences are anaesthetised into coded equality, but it is a useful reminder of the power and lasting effect of a name and the complex web of kinship and religion it can sit within. In rural Mexico, children were only called by nicknames because it is believed they could be harmed by sorcerers who learned their real names; in Cancuc (Mexico) real names were kept a secret to such an extent that some adults never learned their own names! The superstition is that one day the child will grow up to become its name and that knowing someone's name give us control over them. Call someone Ghengis or Big Ears or Satchmo and then they and we have a lot to live up or down to. The name can stick and the dream or insult can backfire or suddenly become the name of someone in the news like a serial killer.

The Chinese system is subtle. Their children are given a carefully conceived name, the meaning of which may be known only to the parents, but they are also given new names at later stages of life: starting school, getting married, beginning a career. Also families have a generational name based on a poem with no repeating words, each generation taking the next word in the poem.

Surnames we take for granted but these have always been particularly important to the Chinese. So important that they put it before their personal name, and however many new personal names, new identities and new skins they acquire, the surname does not change. It is passed down the male line (as it is in the West), although traditionally two people with the same name were not allowed to marry.

In Japan, people were once given new names for new states – such as when they moved house or even when they died, and in the Amazon, Yanamo tribal people have a system whereby every alternate generation is given the same name. A child is named after the living grandparent with prefix Big ... and Little ... But as you can't be named after someone who has died, if a war suddenly occurs, whole generations appear to disappear as a name vanishes.

All very complex. But another useful reminder that names and dynasties and families and religions have power and it is crucial to find the correct labels to fit our identities; also particularly important to recognise in times of rapid change that identity need not be permanent. Witness the currency of virtual names on the Internet.

Stages to consider when naming a child

For most of us the new crucial developments in genetic engineering, and their implications for "identity" are still in the realm of science fiction. Ideas develop so rapidly that we become heady with the implications. We need earthing.

Fortunately, most babies are still created via conventional, natural and traditional means although our procedures for naming, are largely outmoded. Today there is new knowiedge about the development and identity of babies but we still tend to hand out ready made arbitrary labels willed upon us by media, fashion or religion.

The Freudian mythology that a child's ego formation only began between two and four is outdated. Now we know that our ultimate identities are deeply affected by what happens to us in the womb, at birth, and in the first six months of post natal existence as well as by our genetic imprinting and subsequent upbringing, education and adult experiences. Knowing this we could be more subtle, or more informed about when, how and why we welcome and/or name a baby.

Concentration on the biological stages of a baby's development from conception via birth to learning to speak and walk is a salutary consciousness raising exercise. Even if we don't actually give the child a new name at each stage (although it might be fruitful to imagine some), the thought process helps us focus on the mystery and joy of reproduction and the special complexity of each growing individual with their various identities.

Conception

There is some speculation that even in the very first weeks, perhaps even hours, after conception, the fertilised ovum possesses some kind of self-awareness. Psychiatrists who regress patients to pre-birth times report on experiences that appear to go back as far as conception:

I am a sphere, a balloon. I am hollow, I have no arms or legs, no teeth, I don't feel myself to have a front or a back, up or down. I float, I fly, I spin. Sensations come from everywhere. It is as though I am a spherical eye.

from **The Secret Life of the Unborn Child** by Dr Thomas VERNY with John Kelly, 1987, Sphere Books, London

The early embryo

An embryo's growth is affected by the parent's habits. Tobacco, alcohol, drugs and caffeine are absorbed directly through the mother's bloodstream as are anxiety provoking hormones. The mother's state of mind is affected by her support network, her self-confidence and access to love, affection and hope. Poverty, insecurity, tense relationships, and the stresses of our culture can generate anxiety which will affect the well-being and identity of a child, long before birth. As a neurotic society will eventually cause some children to be born with behaviour problems, our baby welcoming ceremonies (or ceremonies when the baby is brought into society) might acknowledge this.

Three months

It is generally believed that once the foetus has matured to the second three months then its ego begins to function as its nervous system starts to become capable of transmitting sensations to its higher brain centres.

Hearing, for example, is one of the first senses we develop and it is one of the last to go. It was certainly during the second half of my wife's pregnancy that my son learned to play the trombone. He is now an excellent professional musician. It was in a beach bar in North Devon. The full Mike Westbrook Orchestra blasting out, in front of a window with their backs to the setting sun. A sun as huge as Sue's belly. Inside her womb Daniel kicked in time and I could feel him dancing under my hand.

Six months

From six months after conception the child's central nervous system becomes more capable of receiving, processing and encoding messages. A neurological memory is then present although there also seems to be evidence of extra neurological memory possibly laid down much earlier in individual cells. If this is the case it gives new credence to Jung's theories of a common collective unconscious and Sheldrake's work on morphogenetic fields which he describes as "The mystery of the coming-into-being of form".

Good to imagine that our howling new Western individual baby, despite being well on the way to Mothercare and other consumer institutions, may be connected through the collective unconscious, to other babies in the world being born (and often dying) at the same time.

Grassroots Post-Modernism by Gustavo ESTEVA and Madhu Suri PRAKASH, 1998, Zed Books, London

One of the sacred cows of modernity is the myth of the individual self ... All that contemporary communitarians seem to be conceiving or offering are devices and techniques for plugging the contemporary individual self into social constructs which create the illusion of 'interpersonal connectedness'.

We really are in it together.

Birth

Opinions differ about the merits of home and hospital birthing, with access to medical expertise and machines and emergency oxygen, but whatever system we follow, it can have a profound effect on the baby and mother. Even seeing one's baby on a scanner screen can provoke a too early sense of mother and child separation.

The long term psychological effects on the subsequent adult of an extended labour or the use of forceps, or premature or Caesarean birth are acknowledged. A recent article in the British Medical Journal, reported on Woman's Hour February 22nd 1999 for instance, mentions a statistical correlation between some difficult births and some subsequent suicides.

The nature versus nurture debate is an old one of course, and the exact balance between genetics and environment both in and out of the womb is very complex. But in a few cases there seem to be links between a difficult birth and for example dyslexia, or hyperactivity or even schizophrenia or heart disease. If a child is born before thirty-two weeks there can be neurological immaturity which can affect the child or adult's personality later on. As there is a tendency now, particularly in the USA, for increased intervention in the birth process, we should at least be aware of the good and bad long term effects this may have on the child, the mother and their relationship.

Keeping a precise diary of the sequence and nature of events from conception to birth could, in the future, be invaluable to us and our children and their counsellors. Whether it is included as part of a naming or birthing ceremony or not, such knowledge (backed up by medical records) should be automatically preserved. Maybe the story with relevant timetable could be annotated in a special "Fact and Photo" Scrapbook and handed over to the child, with due ceremony, when appropriate.

If, as is becoming increasingly clear, our minds are indeed formed by events much earlier in pre-natal existence than was previously imagined, then let's have ready access to that information.

Our suggestion that such attention to the key points in a baby's development could underpin any moment or occasions for naming may be too much but it makes the process more child-centred and helps us question naming habits and customs which may become irrelevant in the next century.

We might decide for instance that the child's early years are so changeable and transitory that it would be better to have a temporary name only for that period and find the real name to reflect the emerging personality of one's offspring, when the right time comes. Maybe even when the child is older it could formally rename itself.

There are also many other key transition points when the *right* name might be discovered. To return to Mexico again, there was once a ritual when, after Maya children have been carried on their mothers' backs for some time, they become old enough to sit on the mother's hip. The purpose of this ritual was not to name but to endow the children with the faculties and skills the parents wanted them to possess. And it comes at a point of course when the child's head is strong enough to be self-supporting.

Humble food is put into the child's mouth that he may learn to adapt himself to whatever difficult circumstance he may have to experience in later ilfe; agricultural implements are placed in his tiny hands so that he may become a good farmer. A gun put into his hands and fired in his presence will make him a good hunter. If it is a girl, the mano for grinding corn, a needle, scissors or spindle is put into her hands.

The ceremony is performed in the domestic oratory with the family and godparents present. Offerings of food are placed on the altar and the implements for the child on the ground. The godmother, holding the child, kneels and repeats prayers three times.

Then she sits the child on her own hip, making a circuit of the space as she puts his hands on each of the implements in succession, and affectionately explains the purpose of each one and the value of knowing how to use it. In the case of a boy he is taken to a tree and made to touch a high branch in order that he may be good at climbing and extracting chicle.

The ceremony develops further with specific foods representing a whole metaphysical system of memory and meaning.

We have already noted that arcane and archaic peasant systems, particularly ones that reinforce negative stereotypes too are not directly relevant to our contemporary society, but the complex detail and method of this example does illustrate how some societies have chosen consciously to intermesh their personal and societal values with ceremonial teachings.

In our fragmented culture we could well learn from and even envy such total practice. What could we invent to centre our children within a structure of considered values and reference points which would be equally sustainable for both the child and society? Is there a useful mythology beyond Teletubbies and the Spice Girls? Is it Swampy and Ecology?

Various post-natal stages

After birth there are of course enormous and rapid developments and we could equally find as many stages to mark as before birth. Any one of these points could be as significant for a naming as any other.

Very tiny babies are not sure where they come from or where they are going. Despite the often traumatic entry point of the birth itself there is a maturing continuum from well before birth to well beyond. *The Continuum Concept* – Jean Liedloff's radical book on child rearing – based on her experiences amongst Stone Age Indians of Venezuela, provides a convincing argument that "we in Western Civilization have largely misunderstood our own nature" and demonstrates many reasons why our usual early separation between mother and child can be harmful. LeidIoff challenges many presumptions about work and babyminding and the Western child's route to full consciousness that we assume to be the norm and advocates mothers carrying, holding and sleeping with babies in their arms until they discover sufficient strong independence and literally crawl away (the children that is!). Her theories are quite

The Continuum Concept by Jean LIEDLOFF, Arkana, London, 1989

The real power behind a name

There was once a sad second-hand car salesman who had a little shop forecourt and suffered ulcers and approaching bankruptcy. Next door to his premises was a huge care saleroom with an enormous forecourt – its millionaire boss had a golden Rolls Royce.

One day the sad salesman decided to change his name. In doing so he also changed his fortune (and his ulcers).

His new name was ENTRANCE!

---

extreme but again they do question our normal patterns of child rearing and how we nurture each new self. Among many non-Western people children are carried around a lot and cry less. So it goes.

Renaming yourself now

Many adults are unhappy with their names. Some years ago I was facilitating a workshop on funerals. We were considering how, adequately, to celebrate the complex identity of a deceased person and how very often this is hampered by the funeral industry. To clear our thinking I proposed an exercise: "If appropriate, send a card to your friends to tell them you are changing your name to whatever".

Two thirds of our group (who happened to be nearly all women) really wanted to change their name. They made cards and presented them publicly in a little ceremony. There was much emotion and rejoicing.

I suspect many more people would do this given the opportunity. It's easy. Just do it. Then if you wish it to be permanent, you can confirm it easily and relatively quickly and legally by Deed Poll.

What's in a Ceremony?

from **How, Then, Shall We Live?** by Wayne MULLER, 1996, Bantam Books, New York, 1996

If you have acquired a name one way or another, why bother with a ceremony? Ceremonies and rituals aren't always appropriate. They can be expensive, boring and irrelevant, only used by authority figures, priests and celebrants to gain control and make money. But they can be exciting, life enhancing and fun as well, putting us in touch with friends, community and deeper layers of ourselves that we often don't acknowledge.

"Being in community with others is an inescapable part of a full and meaningful life. Gathering to observe ritual, ceremony, parade, pilgrimage, festival, these are the ways we remember the rhythm of things, the triumph of the spirit, the cycle of birth and death, the deepening of a life together."

To recap, a naming ceremony is for the child, the parent(s) and the community. For the child the name is a legality but the ceremony is an affirmation to look back on. For the parents it is a public declaration for witnessing. And for both congregation and parents it is an occasion to share. A celebration, with family, friends, neighbours and tribe confirming agreed social and religious values.

The first ceremony most people think about when asked about baby naming is a christening. This usually takes place within a few weeks or months of the birth.

With a carved font, a sympathetic priest, an approving baby, a lace christening shawl, a leak-proof nappy, and Godparents who believe and agree to continue supervising the upbringing of their charge in the Christian faith, it can be very special ... for Christians.

Of Water and Spirit by Malidoma PATRICE SOME, G P Putman & Sons, New York

Some of us have grown up frightened by the superstition that we or our children won't get to heaven unless they have been christened in this way. In the book *Of Water and Spirit* by Malidoma Patrice Some there is a moving and detailed description of such psychic terror imposed on French West Africans by white missionaries, including their imposition of the name French West Africans.

However, as it is possible for most of us to recover from such colonisation and as now only one in four children are baptised, it's time to examine other possibilities. Anthropological textbooks are as full of wild creative ideas for this rite, or series of rites, as they are for funerals.

"The Huichols, for example, perform a "cleansing" and naming ceremony five days after the child is born. At night, while the shaman sings, the name the child is to bear is revealed to him. At dawn, the baby is brought in and the midwife washes it lightly with sacred water and brushes it with the shaman's plumes. When the Sun has risen, both mother and child are bathed in warm water. Then the shaman announces what the child will be called. The navel cord is buried under a century plant, there to live forever. A few months later the child is taken by the parents on a long pilgrimage to sacred caves to be washed by springs representing the Mother of the Gods, Father Sun, Goddess of Corn and the Goddess of the Eastern Clouds. After bowls of water are poured over the naked protesting child (thus insuring the blessings of the springs of the valley), the parents leave gifts for the Goddess which used to be arrows and little heads made of tamale dough.

In Oxchuc, Chiapas, a child is named during the first month, preferably the last week. The parents invite a celebrant who knows the prayers to perform the ceremony. It has to take place on a Friday and the celebrant has to fast for three days. On Thursday night he sleeps in the parents' house. The next morning, at about 6.00 am, he prays before the small domestic altar which has been adorned with pine needles and flowers, on which he places five large and three small candles. Generally the name is selected by the father after some dead member of the family. After the ceremony, a breakfast of boiled eggs, tortillas and beans is served, during which several bottles of liquor are consumed."

from
Mexican Folkways by Frances Toor, Banana Books, New York, 1985

We witnessed a naming ceremony in the village of Saiwan in Bali in 1979 (see page 44). Although on the other side of the world from Mexico, there were many similar features. The moment for the ceremony was very suddenly deemed astrologically auspicious (it was about 3.00 am) and two specialist celebrants were hired. First a woman who prayed with a small congregation of us and two dozen villagers, and after anointing her with oil and water pierced the little girl's ears with gold earrings; then a male Dalang or Shadow Puppet Master performed selected scenes from the Ramayana (a traditional Hindu Epic tale about Gods and Goddesses) to a village gathering. Considerable feasting followed.

In these examples, a special place, day and hour were chosen, an officiant facilitated with traditional knowledge, links were made with the epic pattern of wider natural forces (represented by personified gods) and anointing with water or oil, candles and feasting was common.

It is not always good to lift from other ceremonies, particularly those evolved over many years in rural

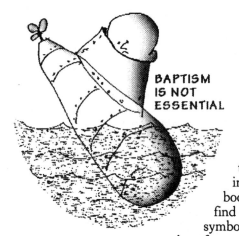

BAPTISM
IS NOT
ESSENTIAL

peasant societies. It is very easy for us to end up with a ceremony which feels fake primitive and is self-consciously and uncomfortably pagan or bizarre. And for other cultures to feel we are appropriating or even colonising their wisdom. On the other hand – now that we have so much information given to us via books and television – we can find our own equivalent of these symbols and methods, provided the references are used with caution. Often the imagery is universal and can still strike a chord with even the least sophisticated of western urbanites.

For instance:

■ Water is a basic component of life. We came from water.

■ A place that has the power of rocks and weather can still our wittering.

■ Dishes of food along with alcohol sustain us.

■ Nakedness of the child (provided it doesn't get pneumonia in our climate) removes decorative frippery and takes us back to the simple beginning we all had.

And so on.

The trick is to use the occasion, the truth and the principles of it all, yet rewrite for our own environment – a park, a transport café, a sheltered bower. A bowl of petals from our garden and water from our favourite river are all conceivable and useable.

It is the essence of our humanity to celebrate our being. To mark our joy in the company of others. We are all creative and can discover our own poetry. It is as simple as that.

Mythology and Beyond

The king cobra, the most deadly snake in the world, has no parental nurturing. Baby snakes are conceived in one three hour coupling; the resulting six or seven white, leathery egg sacks are buried above ground in a leafy nest lassoed together by the mother; she then slides off for ever, leaving each sack full of a dozen tiny snakes to be born and develop on their own. From a tiny haversack of glutinous protein a playfully fighting knot of writhing yellow emerges. Another generation has come into being.

Human conception, birth and growing up has up to now been traditionally altogether different, but it is now conceivable that with artificial insemination, implanted eggs, laboratory foetuses, the reconstructions of genetic patterns through chemical and electronic engineering, we can self-consciously manipulate our own evolution. The well-worn trio of passion, bed and chance may soon be as old-fashioned as gooseberry bushes and we, like the cobra, may choose to separate breeding and nurturing.

Extraordinary events are occurring. In September 1990 the first successful human recipient of gene therapy was a four year-old girl with an inborn defect of her immune system who was "repaired" through copies of the "correct" gene being inserted in her white blood cells. By 1994 the genetic defects responsible for cystic fibrosis, muscular dystrophy, Huntington's Chorea and a form of inherited breast and ovarian cancer had all been identified. At completion of the three billion dollar Human Genome project scientists will have identified every single gene in human DNA and we may soon be able to predict even eye colour and intelligence. Already drug companies are patenting our genes to sell back to us and pigs are breeding with sufficient human genes to avert rejection when their organs are transplanted to humans.

These scary wonders throw up questions about naming and identity. When does human life actually start? Who decides the genetic well-being of our offspring and when? Will it be those who can afford either the genes or the pigs storing their spare parts? Where do the human and animal cross over and what rights do we have over other species? How long should we prolong our lives? If a child born in the west today could survive for 130 years (which is well over twice as long as almost anyone in 1900 and is nearly three times as long as many people in West Africa now), how do we perceive longevity, identity and our place in the wider universe in the next millennium? Indeed, just how many new identities or names could we have, and who is the person? What is the self?

Heady with questions we cannot ignore it helps to look at other cultural systems. There is a western fallacy that "primitive" people believe some ancestral myth that babies come from the Gods and peasants are ignorant of the process of fleshy intercourse or painful childbirth. This is to misunderstand the role of stories in rural cultures. Peasants and nomads know only too well the realities of birth and death and consciously invent other dreamtimes to connect the unfathomable with the unspeakable.

Myths provide structures of value. Models to temporalise, personalise and dramatise the universal facts of existence with symbols and metaphors, giving us a sense of comprehensible connection, a meaning and place to be, between time and the timeless.

Ancient hunting people learned the ways of dangerous but edible wild beasts. Their Gods were half human, half animal, depicted in cave paintings, totems and creation myths with elaborate masks and costume skins. Tribes organised to survive and share the wilderness and their knowiedge of animal nature was profound.

Farmers on the other hand identified with their crops and the soil of the earth. The life rituals of planting and reaping were identified with those of human procreation, birth and maturity so that their Gods favoured elaborate dances, processions and songs acted out in seasonal rhythm.

As both hunters and farmers achieved more stability, social cohesion and control on Earth they looked to the stars, evolving wondrous pantomimes of sacred planets cavorting with the Sun-God and Moon-Goddess in fabulous array. And so forth.

Inevitably there is no going back. As Joseph Campbell said in *The Hero with a Thousand Faces*:

There is no such society any more as the gods once supported. The social unit is not a carrier of religious content, but an economic-political organisation. Its ideals are not those of the hieratic pantomime, making visible on Earth the forms of heaven, but of the secular state, in hard and unremitting competition for material supremacy and resources. Isolated societies, dream bounded within a mythologically charged horizon, no longer exist except as areas to be exploited. And within the progressive societies themselves, every last vestige of ritual, morality and art is in full decay.

from **The Hero with a Thousand Faces** by Joseph Campbell, New York, 1948

But as the old myths or religious symbols break down, many of us would still value some frame to hang on to. But what *do* we meditate upon in our speedy magpie culture of capitalist consumerism? Although many fathers do now participate in the birth of their children, unlike our ancestors we experience few births and few deaths at first hand. We have handed some part of the old realities over to screen equivalents, media gossip and professional experts who do the dirty for us whether it is undertakers, ambulance crews, professional midwives or soldiers, and so forth.

We are losing touch with primary experience. In our anxiety to be educated and civilised we pursue the cerebral, sanitise the animal in us and reserve physical energy for sex, sport and gardening. Birthing and burial,

The Rapid Development of Reproductive Technology

1960   The Pill separates sex and reproduction.

1978   The first test tube baby. In vitro fertilisation (IVF) means that a woman can carry in her womb a child to which she bears no genetic relationship.

1985   Britain's first surrogate mother was paid to have an American couple's baby.

1987   South African woman gave birth to her daughter's triplets (as ma and grandma).

1991   The Human Fertilisation and Embryology Act regulates the technology.

1992   A 61 year old Italian woman gives birth.

1994   Neil and Gillian Clark bear a girl whose sex they had selected before conception.

See Tom Wilkie's "Genes 'R' Us" in **FutureNatural**, ROBERTSON, MASH, TICKNER, BIRD, CURTIS and PUTNAM (eds), Routledge, London, 1996

even hunting, growing food, baking and sharing bread, the everyday focus of other generations and other peoples, come unexpectedly upon most of us. As our cerebral understanding of childbirth increases (images of babies being born are common on television and websites), our sense of its visceral and life-threatening nature evaporates and we hand over even more of the process to doctors, nurses and scientists. Sympathetic and life-enhancing they may well be as individuals; but the impersonal multinational conglomerates and states who employ them may have other ideas. Under the domination of Mammon, Glaxo-Wellcome replaces Hera and Hesta. The National Health Service becomes GOD.

What pattern or contemporary myths are we to seek and what is the orientation of our identity?

If we are seeking new technicians of the sacred, questors of "what it still means to be human", and if this book presumes the purpose, value and form of celebration, ceremony and ritual to be the comprehension and enrichment of our existence, then we must look at all the stages of the human cycle and how these reflect or determine, or are determined by, the co-evolution of us, on Earth and in the Universe.

To make this more concrete, if we decide (for example) that conception, bearing, birthing and the first year of a child's life are significant (if not extraordinary or even miraculous) nodes of human development, then how and why do our ceremonies mark them and in particular with what values, aspirations or dreams are they inculcated. What do we need for our individual and collective practical and spiritual journey?

What is the human equivalent of the cobra's tiny collective knapsack of embryonic protein? What did Dick Whittington need for his journey? If his knotted 'kerchief had been intended to last until 2100 before he turned again, what would we put in beyond a golden sovereign and a jam butty?

A hundred years ago if we had opened out the buckskin travelling pouch of a young North American male Indian we would have found salted buffalo, arrowheads and secular functional objects, but the other half of the contents would have been sacred fetishes, feathers, amulets and bunches of sage. How would our values be signified today if we were to offer a new born Western baby a long lasting holdall with sustenance for their life's journey? Would Whittington and Black Elk both today substitute their knobbly branches for aluminium antennae, preferring solar batteries, radio transmitters and laptops, modems and digital encyclopaedia for dreaming and connecting through cyber space?

WE NAME THIS CHILD STAN LAUREL

A Balinese Naming Ceremony

There are a number of ceremonies that must happen following the birth of a child in Bali: (1) 3 days after birth – feast; (2) 42 days after first bath – feast; (3) 105 days after birth – Naming (described below); (4) 210 days after birth – first birthday. In March 1979 John Fox, Sue Gill and their children Daniel and Hannah (then aged 10 and 8), stayed for 5 weeks with the trainee puppet master in Sawan, Bali and were privileged to observe this Naming ceremony.

For the previous 3 weeks, the women of the household and female neighbours begin nightly to work in groups, preparing the offerings. One night they are folding strips of palm leaves into a small offering and securing them with a section of the leaf spine. Inside is a tiny pinch of something – probably grated coconut. Another night they make plaited and woven baskets out of split leaves, or clipped feather shapes in precise clusters, or fringed fronded displays. The intricate designs are laid down, everyone knows them.

Gede's mother makes more offerings. Out of dyed, cooked rice, she makes sets of 6 images, on banana leaf squares. Orange, pink, yellow and vivid turquoise. The dye – Gudrang – comes in tiny paper packets. Such intense colours, that a pinch of powder colours a couple of big handfuls of rice. On one square the 6 archetypal images are placed in a circle, and this pattern is repeated several times. In addition, each set has a couple of special leaves, a few petals, banana slices and oranges. These have an immediate, short-term purpose – they will be put on the ground out in the street that evening, to allay bad demons.

At the same time, long term preparations are under way for the Naming. Dyed rice squares are being made – thin squares of rice paste on a leaf, gently heated over the fire, to dry them out. These squares will later be fried in coconut oil, to expand. They are not for eating just for visual effect.

One week to go and it is the day for making the special cakes. A dozen women assemble about 6.30am, and begin working with the rice paste – coloured balls, prepared, steamed and kneaded yesterday, ready for an early start. Probably 100 hours work involved in this stage.

Intricate designs, like the finest piped decorations for wedding cakes, but just modelled, rolled, pinched into shape by rough peasant fingers with no tools or utensils. Infinite invention – over 100 different designs. Each colour is significant, each design has a purpose in the scheme of things. They are all carefully fried, 2 or 3 at a time, in the wok over an open fire out in the yard. People, crabs, scorpions, birds, lotus blossoms, rice, stars, flowers – the points of their universe made manifest. Some intricate assemblages in boxes or shallow trays, some mounted on sticks. Spirals, whorls, shells, lattices.

Out of all this poverty comes astonishing beauty. It's as if they can't help it. Anything they turn their hand to turns out wonderfully. And what hands! Hard, careworn field labourers' hands that chop wood, harvest rice, grate, grind, pound, scrub and scrape, yet still retain the sensitivity to mould and model the most delicate fluted petal forms at lightning speed. Each thing made with exquisite care. And made from nothing. Made with joy, and made together. The women share a sisterhood, clearly apparent through these communal activities. It is the root of everything, the basis from which they have so much to give to each other and to

visitors. Working together making offerings, they are cocooned in their own peace. They don't have a relationship towards their traditions, beliefs, customs - they **are** the traditions and customs and the traditions and customs **are** the people. Neither exists outside the other. They work in a stillness outside of time, where the past is the present, with a vision deeply rooted from infancy.

Preparation of the Feast

Mid-morning, about 25 local men arrive at the house, very smart in sarongs, sashes and turbans. Three men carry wooden trays on their heads, about 4ft long, with several flat logs standing neatly in them. Coffee is served to the men, then they sit crosslegged on the outside raised platforms in symmetrical rows, facing each other across the trays. Each has his own knife (some are ceremonial knives with brass finish to the handles), and use the log as a chopping block in the communal tray. They begin to chop garlic and tiny onions – it sounds like a drumming band and is treated as a solemn procedure. Each man chops fast, eyes down, no talking, in unison for 25 minutes. Tremendous manpower for what seems like a few inconsequential onions, chopped until you can hardly see them.

The kids are sent running to and fro to fetch bricks, a tall brick fireplace gets built and is set going immediately with a huge wok on top. In the household temple a bricklayer with mortar and spirit-level is starting to construct a new ancestor shrine.

Slaughtering and roasting meat is men's business. The women arrive a bit dishevelled at times, breast feed babies, while they continue weaving and plaiting, deal with infants, laugh and gossip and sit in anarchic unstructured groups, tossing stuff to and fro as they need it, or have finished it.

At the same moment that we first lay eyes on Christina (the legendary new baby girl for whom the Naming ceremony will be held) we hear the screams of the first pig being killed for the feast, just three paces away.

Time to chop the meat. It is jointed and then a small piece is given to each man for chopping into a kind of mince/puree. Over one fire, fat is being rendered down, over another a stock is being boiled, with vegetables and pieces of skin on bamboo spines, for easy retrieval later.

The two suckling pigs are on spits down where the flour is pounded, roasting over mounds of coconut husks. Kebabs are being made, and lumps of fat are chopped into grated coconut.

The parents of the new baby are not involved in any of this. Mother sits writing out an expenditure list at the table. She's a midwife, Chinese, and is the only woman in western dress. She arrives with quilted nylon bottle warmers, sterile flask of boiled water, special cups and plates for baby. This place must be a nightmare for her. Her son of three is the only child with shoes, and without head lice.

The house has been full to bursting with offerings since yesterday, which was the big finishing-off day. Special cloths have been pinned up on the walls as a backdrop, and woven mats put down to carpet the floor. The room is long and narrow - maybe 24x8ft. Two rectangular tables have been set at one end, one on the left, one on the right, leaving merely a narrow 2ft wide passageway between them. The tables are loaded with offerings piled high – food, foliage, fruit, incense, spices, and once it was cold, a whole roast suckling pig and other cooked meats. In the temple, all the shrines are draped with white, yellow or black and white cloths.

Overture

The arrival of the Dalang and his retinue is imminent and the big feast is due to start. The Dalang is a kind of lay priest. He is the puppet master, and on this occasion has been invited to the village, and paid for by Gede's family, to give the Wayang (the ritual entertainment appropriate to the Naming) in the form of a public performance of the shadow play for everyone to see, in the market place.

Feast

Seated on the floor around the perimeter of the room are honoured guests and friends. No women allowed. At the outside kitchen about 15 women in best sarongs and lace tops hover in the wings, waiting for the signal to carry in the spread. The best food – choice cuts of chicken, duck and pork, kebabs, stuffing, blood puddings, sweet and sour pork meat balls ...

Polite social talk and much rapid eating from the men, dessert, coffee, cigarettes, then departure to begin the shadow puppet show in the village. The women do a quick wash-up for the second sitting – guests Grade II – then finally they themselves eat about 9pm (Many had worked through the previous night and all day without rest).

To get to the performance it is necessary to run the gauntlet of bamboo cannons exploding in the street. Coconut oil was burning in the lamp behind the screen, which gives a flickering light and gives to the puppets a pulsating and vibrant quality. (The oil is from coconuts from Gede's garden, laboriously extracted by his mother after hours of grating and simmering. The residue fattens the pig for the feast. The husks fuel the cooking fires – a totally integrated system – art, life, religion ... no divisions). The Dalang has a deep resonous voice (part of the training is a diet of special roasted bananas), and is accompanied by the gonerh – a small bamboo orchestra.

"The dalang and the puppets, the gamelan, the banana trunk that holds the puppets, the screen, the lamp – all are invited into one being. The dalang is life itself. The body, acting and speaking, is the puppet appearing on the screen of the world and moved by that life, the dalang. The entering of the suksina (soul) into the body is the entering of the dalang into the puppet. So we are all dominated by the suksina in us, which is life itself. Our life story is the plot of the wayang. We are the spectacle ourselves. Who is the spectator? The spectator is the witness of all that lives ..."

Wiratjapa, a wandering Javanese mystic

The audience are constantly moving around, eating, smoking, sleeping, talking, laughing, going off to a stall for coffee, but they never lose the thread of the story. They already know all the stories and roles inside out, and do not need to play the role of audience to follow in the western sense. This 3000 year old mythology applies to today; it is living and dynamic. The Gods themselves – not their shadows – are on the screen.

After the performance – approximately 3 hours – all the puppets have to be packed away in a box, except for the three highest deities: Shiva; Brahma; and Vishnu.

Holy Water

Holding these three leather puppets, the dalang prepares to make the holy water necessary for the Naming. The dalang recites formulas and offers prayers to each one, over a jar of water put before him. He recites the calendar months – naming the day, the occasion – and asks for blessing for the Naming. The water will be taken back to the house for the Naming, which will begin after the dalang has rested and departed.

Naming Ceremony

At midnight the Naming begins. This is to be conducted by the offering-maker, not by a priest. The offering-maker may be a male or female – in this case it is a woman. There are 3 of them in Sawan and they receive a fee for their services - discreetly given after the event in the form of money inside an offering

which is taken to their house. They act in an advisory capacity beforehand. The baby's grandmother has made previous visits to the offering maker, to be instructed on preparations.

On the day she had come to the house about noon, but did not come into her own until midnight. She is a dignified old woman, who looks immensely wise, gentle and kind – but so do most of the old women in Bali – each in her own way marked by different degrees of world-weariness. Setting her apart from these women she had an extra quality about her – an ease and quiet command of the situation, a natural authority to do the job. That authority sprang from her own deep centre to her being – her personal centre became the pivot of the whole ceremony for all of us. In a room, a space, her presence created a special climate, an aura around her – whilst the smile behind her eyes made her totally approachable.

Part One

The ceremony begins inside the house – prayers and offerings to the Gods, asking them to protect the child. The offering maker sits under a kerosene lamp on a chair in a narrow gap between the two tables groaning with offerings, including a double effigy of the child – one plaited out of banana leaves (tropical corn dolly), the second painted in white on dried bark. The atmosphere is rich and heavy. She begins by touching and handling the offerings.

Picking up, one at a time, ornate silver bowls loaded with tropical fruits, leaves and hand made symbols and confections, and says a prayer over each one. As one is put down, the next is picked up. This is private prayer and takes maybe half an hour.

Then she calls upon the child's "Five Brothers": Blood, Placenta, Water, Umbilicus and The Human Spirit. She calls for them in the order in which they appeared during the child's birth. If the waters broke first, water is the eldest brother.

The offering maker picks up two clumps of dried brown leaves, each tightly bound, holding one in each hand. These had been made some weeks before. The Balinese believe that everyone is born on Earth as a punishment. Another woman takes a knife and firmly cuts the bands on each bundle of leaves, symbolising the releasing of pain for the child. Those bundles are dipped in the holy water and used to sprinkle baby and parents several times.

She calls upon the Trinity and as she names the Gods one by one, sticks a few grains of rice onto the face of the baby and her parents. For Shiva, the Destroyer (former of breath which is the link between the body and the soul), the most powerful God – rice goes in the centre of the forehead. For Brahma, the Creator (former of bones, flesh, nerves and body temperature), rice goes on the right temple. For Vishnu, the Guardian (former of blood, marrow, fat, glands and the body fluids, which give life to the whole human frame), rice goes on the left temple.

Short lengths of very soft spun string are cut and placed across the crown of the head and tied round each wrist, again, baby first, then mother and father in turn. This is to wish blessings on the child: "May you have bones like steel, sinews like wire ..."

All this time the parents are seated on chairs near the offering maker, mother holding the child, who is awake and alert and peaceful. The immediate group of women involved, other onlookers, men and the odd child numbered about a dozen and sit on mats on the floor towards the back of the room. It has been a long day. Some are fast asleep; another man, flat on his back, is absorbed in a paper comic strip!

All the time three of the seated women are singing an endless chant/ drone. One is a lively old crone who keeps interjecting her cackles of laughter. The trio occasionally get the words mixed up, or one will start on the wrong note and the whole chorus dissolves into laughter. Just outside the door the gonerh is playing – three musicians relatively inexperienced, so they play the same thing over and over again, but it doesn't matter.

The atmosphere is quite relaxed. The baby occasionally pees and Dad gets up and goes to the bedroom for clean knickers. The glass feeding bottle, with pink plastic hygienic cover, stands incongruously on the edge of the offerings table – the only thing that makes us sure we are still in the 20th century.

Outside at 2am

The Balinese are strongly influenced by the spirits of rice, trees, rocks, rivers, the Sun, the rain, mountains ... often these are malevolent spirits and almost daily offerings are made to them. Offerings are now made so the demons do not disturb the baby.

The singers have been going for 2½ hours now, and are getting tired. From time to time the women who have freely given scores of their hours' labour in making offerings for the ceremony appear. They look over the wall, jeering in good natured fashion. "Call that singing?" Laughter punctuates everything.

Gifts

At the side, placed on a block is a bowl of water with two small plaited offerings of fresh green leaves. This symbolises the river. Six women get to their feet, each takes a different object, and they walk in a circle three times, dipping their object into the water each time they pass the bowl. The objects include the two child effigies, a long leaf, and a special purplish fruit studded with jewellery. This is gifts of gold and silver given to the child on the occasion of its Naming (similar to our silver christening mug and spoon).

All the jewellery is put into the basin of holy water. Grand-mother takes the baby and piece by piece she is adorned with it: tiny gold chain bracelets for each wrist; a tiny gold ring for the middle finger of each hand; a gold anklet; a long gold chain pendant necklace and two solid silver ankle bracelets. A small white cloth is put over the baby's dress, as a sarong, and some yellow cloth as a tiny ceremonial sash over the top.

Ear Piercing

Grandmother holds the child, another woman's confident hand holds the the head firm into grandmother's empty breast, and the baby's mother opens her sterile jars, takes out swabs and a long needle, and in a matter-of-fact fashion pierces the earlobe and inserts a gold earring. It is repeated for the other side and finished off with blobs of antiseptic cream. Jokes about whether or not the hole on the left is level with the one on the right.

As a final act, all the remaining holy water is sprinkled – through a sort of colander woven from leaves – over the baby and her parents. By the end they are quite drenched.

Conclusions

All the offerings are picked up off the ground, and at 3am a procession goes off to the river, to throw everything in. Not to waste a trip to the river, each woman takes an empty can and comes back carrying 5 gallons of water on her head. The next day is scheduled as a no work day. No cooking – plenty of cold pork to eat up – and no water will be carried, so this ceremonial procession turns into a domestic expediency on its return.

Mythology of Childbirth

Ceremonies to name and welcome a newly born baby
are often designed to protect that child from bad omens
during the first few years of life. For people living in
different cultures around the world, these early years are
a precious and vulnerable time.

History and Superstitions

After giving birth, a mother in Palau who is a follower
of traditional Shinto, will stay alone with her child for
four days. During this time the mother is bathed,
repeatedly, using rebotel leaves, turmeric and coconut
oil. At the end of their seclusion together the new
mother and child are ready to re-enter society. Seclusion
rituals can be seen as a way of protecting the new child
from bad omens. For the mother in Palau, washing
helps protect her from the blood of childbirth which is
believed to be a source of dangerous power.

Traditionally in Japan, the birth of a boy was marked by hanging a paper bag in the shape of a carp on the end of a bamboo pole

In the Yemen, mother and child go into seclusion for as
much as forty days. During this time of bonding, the
child is bound tightly in swaddling
clothes. This recreates the
security of the womb and
keeps the baby protected as
it was before birth. Baby
binding is also practiced
in China, Native
American communities
and Russia.

For the Ainu of Asia, the
seclusion and protection
of the newborn is based on
the idea that it is only after
a few days of 'real life' that
the child becomes a real
individual. The Ainu

believe that the child receives their body from their mother, during pregnancy, and their soul from their father. The soul enters the child in these first few days after birth. Gradually the child becomes a 'whole' being.

Establishing a connection between the child and their ancestors is an important part of many welcoming ceremonies. With the Tshi on the Gulf of Guinea, a newborn child is shown a collection of objects which belonged to dead members of the family. The child's choice connects them with one particular ancestor and they are incorporated into the family. In Northern Australia, Aboriginals mark their passage through life with ceremonies which link them with their ancestors from Creation Time. "Baby Smoking" is the first welcoming ceremony in a child's life. The mother and grandmother will light a fire with twigs, konkerberry branches, crushed dampened bark and green leaves to make a purifying smoke. When the smoke rises, the grandmother will hold the baby and the mother will squeeze her milk into the fire. The child's grandmother will then wave the child through the purifying smoke. With fire, smoke, mothers' milk and grandmother's hands the Aboriginal baby enters life with the multiple blessings of mother Earth and the mothers of his family.

In Catholic Northern Spain, the importance of protecting the baby's first years is given physical representation and a Biblical parallel. The old Biblical story of King Herod is re-enacted. King Herod, when hearing that the "King of Kings" had been born in Bethlehem, ordered all male infants to be killed. In Spain, newborn babies are placed on a mat and, with a crowd of people watching, a man will leap over the mat and the babies. When the man lands safely, just as the baby Jesus escaped Herod's slaughter, so the children escape this moment of danger. The newborn babies survive the hazard and are prepared for a safe and healthy journey through their childhood.

In Britain a pregnant woman was often set apart to protect her and her baby from supernatural influences.

One superstition is that birthmarks are caused and shaped by something which has frightened the mother during pregnancy. In Wales a pregnant woman was not allowed to spin or work in a dairy. In Yorkshire a cradle had to be paid for before it was brought into the home – otherwise the child that slept in it would eventually be 'too poor to pay for its own coffin'.

A common thread in many superstitions is that one should not presume upon future events (eg decorate the nursery, buy the nappies, take delivery of the pram) as this may cause the opposite to take place and events to not work out as predicted. To us, in the modern world, this seems the most unhelpful and depressing kind of belief. However, it is amusing to see it turned around and used in a positive way as in the case of Suffolk folklore which suggested that if a woman did not want another child the best thing she could do was to keep the cradle and items of a previous baby's clothes!

Divination

There are many stories and superstitions which give advice on how best to predict the sex of a baby before it is born.

In Cornwall, it is said that when a boy is born under the waning moon, the next birth will be a girl. When a girl is born under the waning moon, the next will be a boy. However, when a child is born under a waxing moon, the next birth will be of the same sex.

One very popular way to predict the sex of a baby is by using a wedding ring. Suspend a wedding ring, held by a piece of thread, over the palm of the pregnant woman. If the ring swings in an oval or circular motion the baby will be a girl. If the ring swings in a straight line the baby will be a boy.

Boys are alleged to be 'carried high' while girls are 'carried low'. Pregnancies which run for longer than nine months are thought to result in boys because 'they need more effort in the making'. Apparently there is some statistical evidence that pregnancies involving male babies do last longer.

In Wales a sheep's shoulder blade was sometimes scraped clean, scorched, holed, threaded through its thinnest part and hung above the door of the house. The first person to enter the following morning (other than members of the household) would be of the same sex as the future child.

If you're interested in divining the personality of your child then never forget the old poem:

"Monday's child is fair of face;
Tuesday's child is full of grace;
Wednesday's child is full of woe;
Thursday's child has far to go;
Friday's child is loving and giving.
Saturday's child works hard for a living.
But the child that is born on the Sabbath day
is fair and wise, good and gay."

Good Luck for the Child

Ceremonies wishing good luck for a child exist in many forms. Some are performed by the child's parents and closest family, some are expressions of thanks and good wishes by the whole community. In other cases, the children themselves perform ceremonies to protect against bad luck.

In America and Britain, new parents will often smoke a cigar in celebration of the birth of a new child. In Russia they plant a tree. The child's tree is taken very good care of as it is believed that the tree and child are connected. The tree grows with the child and if it flourishes so will the child, but if it dwindles so too will the child. The belief in a connection between the newborn and a tree is common in Germany, France and England as well as

Russia. In Cornish popular superstition it is unlucky for parents to wash the baby's head for the first twelve months and washing a baby's hands before the first birthday will take away future riches.

The Ngente, a Lushae tribe in Assam celebrate new birth together as a whole society. A three day feast is held every Autumn in honour of all the children born that year. The feast brings good luck to all newborn babies. For the first two days of the feast all the adults sit together, eat and drink. On the third day the men, disguised as women, go from house to house calling on the new mothers of the year. The new mothers give them drinks and presents in return for which they dance.

In the Punjab, the child keeps sections of their own hair, nails and umbilical cord to bring good luck into their early life. By keeping these pieces and preventing them from falling into the hands of some other person, the child will be able to keep their own self whole and healthy.

A ritual burying of the placenta is common in many places – frequently a tree may be planted on top of it

When a baby was born in England it was traditional for the female friends of the family to visit the new mother and child during the first couple of weeks. They would all sit around, coo-ing at the new baby and nattering with its mother. This tradition was known as God-sip and the word mutated over the centuries into ... gossip.

How to Carry a Baby

The first pram was built around 1733 by William Kent at Chatsworth in England and designed to be pulled by a dog. It was not until 1850 that they were manufactured in any quantity when two London firms developed three wheelers (which were pushed, by humans, rather than pulled) and intended for children to sit in. Surprisingly not until 1876 was a model

The Lapps "packed" their babies in cases that looked like new moons

invented suitable for a child to lie down in. Apart from a few small wagons used by, for example, working class hop pickers in Kent, the real development of the pram seems to follow the car; one was in fact driven by a petrol engine in the early 1920s.

Old cynics might argue that it's good early training to persuade babies to buy cars. Jean Liedloff might add that it's another part of the plot to disempower mothers and separate the child at a too early stage. Is it the beginning of turning ourselves into helpless luxury loving wheeled consumers or one kind of liberation for women who would otherwise be obliged to carry children on top of everything else they have to carry!

In a fascinating exhibition called "Beloved Burden", mounted by the Tropenmuseum in Amsterdam in 1993 there was a wonderful parade of tableaux depicting baby carrying methods from all round the world. In the words of the catalogue:

"All over the world children are carried, in a sling or in a portable crib. It is a custom as old as humanity, a tradition that in many places is still very much alive. There are only a few places where the tradition has disappeared."

In the past 30 years the tradition has been revived in Western Europe as modern sophisticates have reexamined the wisdom and inspiration of older cultures. Interesting to see how Western families were in the thirties and forties (and unfortunately still are) manipulated into buying very expensive prams as status symbols.

The exhibition was very relevant to naming children. In its infinite variety of ideas from Greenland to Cape Horn, from Siberia to South Africa, from Alaska to Australia, depicting mothers carrying infants on their backs, hips or stomachs, in cribs, cloths, straps or baskets, in every climate, with every conceivable decoration and accompanying toy or magical talisman, it demonstrated how inventive particular and local humans can be and often how much the responsibility for children is shared through the extended family of a tribe. Even the role of the child in the tribe is often signalled through the decoration of the carrying device. If only our namings could be so inventive and so particular to both child, region and metaphysical and economic systems.

Namings around the World

A name for a new baby identifies the child as an individual. It can also express the beliefs and values of a community as well as the parent's hopes for their child in life.

For the Ik, an African tribe on the borders of Uganda and Kenya, the naming ceremony of a new child also celebrates the reunification of the family after a period of separation. After childbirth the father is excluded from the house for a week. At the end of that week paternal grandparents arrive for a feast during which there is ceremonial drinking of millet beer and the child is given a name.

In one Hindu naming ceremony, the child is given two names. One is an ordinary name to be used by people in general. The other is known only to the child's family.

On the third day of the third moon, the father presents the newly named child to that moon. The child is made 'real' to the family, the community and the wider world.

At a Mormon naming ceremony in Salt Lake City, Utah the child receives "The Father's Blessing". The baby's father and close male friends form a tight circle with one hand on a shoulder and another beneath the baby. The father then tells the baby of his hopes and dreams for her, "I bless you with peace and the love of your family. I bless you with happiness in these troubled times. I bless you with the power to see the beauty in this world." Finally, the baby's name is entered into the church register.

In Christian societies children are often given the names of parents and grandparents, but the !Kung of Namibia and also Ashkenazi Jews will never give a child the name of a living parent.

The Lakota Sioux give their newborn a name which they hope will guide the child's life and offer them ideals to live up to. In an ancient naming ceremony, the Blood Indian Elder purifies himself with burning sweetgrass on an altar of clay and glowing embers. Using red ochre dye, he marks the palm of his hand and paints the baby's face with the sign of the tribe. The newborn is held aloft and presented to the Sun so that its power and radiance will be with the child through its life.

The Parsees held a baby over a fire to exorcise any evil spirits

THE TRAVELBAG

Green is for victory
a thin woman returning
I lay it here.

White is the little garment I have made
to clothe thy body
I lay it here.

Fairyflax under my foot
Mothan root under my knee
I lay them here.

Neither hurry nor linger
on your journey. Come steady, come bravely.

Bones open as the
    rock in the mountain
opened. Flesh hold

as the waters held the feet
of the son of god without failing.

Fairyflax under my foot
Ring of bright Mothan
    under my knee
I lay them here.

Jeni Couzyn

PART TWO
TRADITION TODAY

I f you are considering having your child christened then, first, take a moment to understand what the ceremony is all about. If you're a practising member of one of the other four major religions found in Britain today then a brief description of the equivalent ceremony for each can be found in the second half of this section.

Current Christian Practice

Christening

The dictionary definition of the verb "to christen" is "to receive a person, usually an infant, into the Christian Church by baptism; to name a child formally at baptism." Baptism is one of the church's most profound sacraments, that is a ceremony which is the visible form of invisible grace, or the sign of a sacred thing. Jesus himself was baptised by John the Baptist and there is much documentation through the history of the church for this practice. The purpose of christening is to recognise in an outer way the spiritual identity and purpose of a soul. The ceremony welcomes the child into the world and into the family of Christ and blesses its name at the start of its spiritual journey through life. There are different beliefs within the Church about Baptism: some people believe that it is a gift of grace from God; others that Baptism is a reward for good works which should take place only when the person involved is able to take responsibility for his/her own part in the transaction. Most usually the former belief holds true and Baptism is an archetypal celebration of the gift of life itself and a sign of belonging and salvation.

The Service

An important element of the Baptism service is that the child is welcomed into the Christian community so it is important that this is not a private ceremony but one in which there is a congregation to bear witness. For this reason although Baptism can take place as a separate service, it is often included as part of the Communion service or during morning or evening services of prayer. It is also common for several babies to be baptised at once.

Structure

The christening service has several different parts. The exact form and content vary according to the denomination of Christianity, but the basic structure of the ceremony used in the Church of England gives an indication of what takes place:

- Preparation, which greets all those who are going to take part in the ceremony and offers prayers which draw together the hopes and themes of baptism.

- Psalms, readings and teachings (ie a sermon) which are appropriate to the occasion.

- The actual baptism, which involves introducing the children who are going to be baptised and their parents and godparents; asking questions which alert them and the congregation to their responsibilities in what is about to happen; making the sign of the cross on the child's forehead; going to the font where the water is blessed and the three-fold Baptism given by sprinkling with water or total immersion.

- Prayers which sum up the significance of the event.

- The Welcome and Peace during which the baptismal candles are lit and the child is sent out into the world "in the light and peace of Christ".

Symbolism

The christening service uses the symbolism of light, water, oil, clothing and the sign of the cross. Whilst the words of the ceremony contain its meaning these symbols operate at a different level of experience:

Light the central promise made on behalf of the child is a commitment to turn away from the darkness towards the light, and the lighting of the candle represents this process. The baptismal candle can be kept and lit on special occasions in the child's life subsequently.

Water is essential for life and stands for the cleansing and washing away of sins so that the physical washing represents the spiritual cleansing or purification. In some religions baptism involves total immersion in water.

Oil is optional but may be used for anointing the child. There is an old testament tradition that priests and kings were anointed with oil as a sign of their special mission. It is also a reminder of the way that athletes prepare for a contest, using oil to give strength.

Clothing both scripture and tradition suggest that the pure in heart will be recognised by their white clothes so the traditional white christening robe, which is often a family heirloom, passed on from generation to generation, symbolises regeneration and cleansing. In some religions, particularly where there is total immersion, the person is baptised naked and then assumes white clothes as a symbol of rebirth.

Sign of the cross the traditional symbol which indicates sanctity and unity with Jesus Christ.

Why people do it

For many of us birth is a miracle and one of the most profound experiences in life. Baptism is a way of sharing our joy with our family and friends, announcing that this miracle has occurred and that we wish to give thanks for it. For these reasons people who are not Christians themselves ask for baptism for their children. In Christian terms, baptism is a way of receiving the child into the family of Christ through the church and of blessing the child at the beginning of its life's journey and for those who share this faith baptism is a necessity because it answers the deep seated need to engage with God and the Church. There is also a traditional belief that it is necessary to be baptised in order to be saved, as a kind of immunisation against damnation. Whilst this could be regarded as superstition it can be a strong unconscious influence in persuading people to seek baptism for their children.

What contracts are we entering into?

Because the baby is too small to make his or her own promises the parents and godparents act as sponsors

and make those promises on the child's behalf. Fundamentally the vows undertake that the child "will renounce the devil and all his works, and constantly believe God's Holy Word, and obediently keep His commandments". This turning away from the darkness towards the light, or from evil towards goodness is the central tenet of the baptism service and because the child needs to grow towards these promises in his or her life, the godparents promise to teach the Christian beliefs and eventually bring the child to the Bishop for confirmation. If parents feel, for whatever reason, that it is too difficult to enter into these promises it is possible to ask for a service of thanksgiving instead.

Godparents

Within the Christian church godparents are seen as extended family members who will provide spiritual support, guidance and care throughout the child's life and also sponsor him or her at baptism. For these reasons the church requires that the godparents should be more than trusted friends of the family. They should be examples of good Christian living and should have been baptised into the church and also confirmed, though the latter is not absolutely necessary. The Church stipulates that the child should have a minimum of two godparents but preferably three, two of the same sex and one of the other sex.

Traditional gifts

Godparents and other family members give gifts on this occasion. The Church emphasises that these do not have to be expensive, but there is a tradition for giving things which the child can keep for the rest of its life – this may be a silver christening mug or spoon, or a bible or prayer book or some other object of religious significance such as a cross and chain or an appropriate painting.

Christening cake

There is also a tradition that the christening cake which is cut at the party after the baptism service should be the top tier of the parents wedding cake, which has been preserved for this occasion.

Costs

A donation to the church towards the costs of the service is an option. Different churches may ask for particular contributions, but the service is usually free. Apart from this the costs are those associated with the party which usually follows the christening. This is traditionally a christening tea, with cake etc, rather than a sit-down meal, but some people may want to have champagne or wine for celebration.

Practice in Other Religions

Waves of immigration into Britain have brought with them many other traditions. Here is a brief summary of the baby naming practices in the other main religions.

Hinduism

Welcoming
There are 16 traditional steps, called samskar, in the life cycle of a Hindu. Some of the samskar are more often celebrated than others. The first begin before the baby is born with prayers for its health and happiness. Most Hindus perform the fourth samskar when the newborn baby is washed, and then the father may put honey or ghee into the baby's mouth, perhaps using a gold ring, and recite some prayers. In some places the sacred syllable "aum" may be written on the baby's tongue with honey from a special pen. Aum represents the sound of God and creation, containing all the secrets of

the universe, and is recited at the start and end of all prayers, so in this way the child is welcomed spiritually. The father may recite a prayer part of which is as follows:

Dear child, I give you this honey and ghee, which is provided by God, who is the creator of the world. May you be protected by God and live in this world for a hundred autumns. By God's grace may you become strong and firm like a rock, an axe for the wicked, and bright in character. May God give you long life and understanding of the Vedas.'

From the Grihya Sutra

from the Grihya Sutra in **Discovering Sacred Texts: Hindu Scriptures,** Heinemann Educational, London, 1994 copyright of the prayer: V P (Hemant) Kanitkar

It is important to have a priest cast the baby's horoscope as this will be used later in life to decide on lucky times for marriage etc.

Naming

A priest also decides on an auspicious day for choosing a name – sometime before the first birthday, but usually when the baby is 12 days old. A priest is often asked to suggest an initial or syllable. Choosing the right name is felt to be very important in order to bring luck to the child. At the naming ceremony the baby is dressed in new clothes. The name is announced by the eldest woman, and the father says to the baby, 'Now your name is ...'

Everyone sings songs and eats a special sweet made with fruit and nuts. Among some communities, the maternal uncle may feed the child its first spoonful of rice, a formal step towards weaning, so that naming seems to be connected to the first step towards adulthood.

At the time of the sixth samskar, which is the baby's first outing it is exposed to the rays of the Sun. In the West, it is common to take the baby to the mandir, the Hindu temple, where it will be blessed.

The eighth samskar takes place on the first birthday, when, among some Hindus, a boy's head is shaved and a girl's hair is cut. This represents the removal of any bad deeds from a previous incarnation and the start of a new life.

So the baby's life seems to begin not all at once, but to gradually unfold, with the various samskar, during the first year of its life.

Sikhism

Welcoming
The baby is welcomed into the world as soon as possible after birth, by someone saying the first words of the *Guru Granth Sahib*, the holy book; words which sum up the most important features of Sikh belief.

The parents may give sweets or presents to friends and neighbours as they announce the birth, and relatives visit, bringing presents for the baby.

Naming
Children are often given 'pet' names, before they receive their official name, and may continue to be known by this 'pet' name. The official naming ceremony for the baby usually takes place within the first few weeks of its life at a normal gathering in the gurdwara, the Sikh temple. The parents often bring special new pieces of cloth, called rumalas, which cover the holy book, and are also expected to pay for karah parshad, the food which is shared after the service. At the end of the service, there is the usual prayer for guidance, called the Ardas, which can be adapted, in this case to thank God for the gift of the baby. Then the parents lay the baby in front of the holy book which is opened at random by the Granthi, who looks after the book, and the first verse on the left-hand page is read out. The first letter of the verse determines the first letter of the baby's name, which the parents must choose there and then, with help and suggestions from the other people who are present. Since Sikh names may be used for either gender, the name chosen is followed by either Singh, to indicate a boy, or Kaur, for a girl. When the name is announced, everyone shouts the Sikh greeting, 'Sat-Sri-Ahal', which means, 'God is Truth'.

The ceremony where the baby is given amrit may take place here or may have happened earlier at home. Amrit is a mix of sugar and water, made special by being stirred with a two-edged sword called a khanda. To drink amrit from the same bowl symbolises that all are equal members of the faith. In this case a few drops of amrit are placed on the baby's tongue, and the mother drinks the rest, and prayers are said. The following is a hymn for the naming ceremony written by the mother of Guru Arjan.

'Dear Son, this is your mother's blessing. May God never be out of your mind even for a moment. Meditation on God should be your constant concern. It purges people from all faults. May God, the Guru, be king to you. May you love the company of God's people. May God robe you with honour and may your food be the singing of God's praises.'

Adi Granth 486 from **Teach Yourself World Faiths: Sikhism,** Hodder and Stoughton, London copyright of the prayer: W Owen Cole

Islam

Welcoming

As soon as possible after the baby is born the call to prayer and the command to worship are whispered in its ear, which welcomes it into the religious community. These words are, 'Allah is the only God and Muhammad is his true Messenger.'

The Victorian perception of a Persian naming ceremony as illustrated in **The Strand Magazine**

A small drop of honey or piece of sugar may be placed on the baby's tongue, though this has no religious connotations, and the reasons for it are no longer known.

When the baby is seven days old an optional ceremony may be held, called the Aqiqah. In the past a sheep or goat would have been killed, and some of the meat given to the poor. Today money may be given to the poor instead. The child's head is shaved and the amount to be given is based on the weight of the hair in silver, though in some communities, gold may be used as the measure if the baby is a girl. In the event of the baby being bald, an amount is estimated. Olive oil may be rubbed onto the baby's head after it has been shaved.

Circumcision of boys, which usually takes place in the first two or three months, is important in establishing Muslim identity.

Naming
The name may be chosen by the father, the eldest brother, or the elders may be asked to select a name. The name may be selected for personal, family or religious reasons or even because it is popular, but all Arabic names have a meaning. For example, a boy may be given one of the many names of Allah with the prefix of Abd, meaning servant; therefore 'Servant of God.'

Judaism

Welcoming
A boy is circumcised usually within the first eight days of his life, to show that he has entered into the covenant of Abraham, but circumcision will be delayed if the child is ill. Circumcision takes place at home, in the presence of male relatives and witnesses. The father pronounces the benediction;

'Just as he has been initiated into the covenant, so may he be initiated into the study of the Torah, to his nuptial canopy and to the performance of good deeds.'

A feast follows, since this is a joyful occasion.

Naming

The child is given a Hebrew name in addition to a first name and surname from the surrounding culture. The Hebrew name consists of a first name, followed by 'son of' or 'daughter of', and then either the mother's or father's name, or both. The first name is usually chosen to remember a dead person from within the family. Since the written Hebrew uses consonants, it is possible to vary the vowels, eg a daughter might be called Selma after a grandfather called Shlomo.

A girl's name is usually registered at a synagogue immediately after the birth. The Hebrew name is used as well as their ordinary name and is especially important at religious ceremonies. If a baby dies it is still important to give it a name, so that at the resurrection it will be able to recognise its parents.

According to **The Strand Magazine** the Banians – an Indian trading class – used to toss the baby with a quantity of rice for 15 minutes before the infant's sister gave it any name which she thought proper!

HEARTSONG

I heard your heartbeat.
It flew out into the room, a startled bird
whirring high and wild.

I stopped breathing to listen
so high and fast it would surely race itself
down and fall

but it held strong, light
vibrant beside the slow deep booming
my old heart suddenly audible.

Out of the union that holds us
   separate
you've sent me a sound like a
   name.
Now I know you'll be born.

Jeni Couzyn

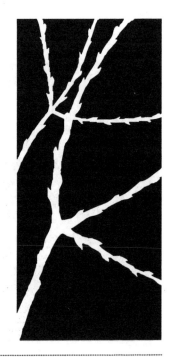

PART THREE
WHAT TO DO WHEN
A NEW PERSON IS BORN

You'll probably have been thinking about names for months when your child is born. Then all of a sudden it's "make-your-mind-up" time. We look at what you absolutely have to do in the section below, then later in this part there are some background thoughts on choosing a name.

Some Law

What you have to do

In the UK it is a parental responsibility to register a child's birth within 42 days of the event (Births & Deaths Registration Act 1953, section 2). The birth must be registered in the district in which it took place although it can be possible for a registrar from another district to take the details and forward them.

Not registering

We heard of a couple who lived on a smallholding in the 1980s and whose son, Zen, was not registered by them. Somehow the hospital notified the authorities and they were taken to court – the outcome was that they were told to comply with the law and sent home. As far as we know they ignored the court order and no further action was taken against them.

If the parents are legally married then only one of them need attend (details of the marriage will be required but not necessarily the marriage certificate itself). In this case the baby is assumed to be a child of the marriage and husband and wife will be named as father and mother.

If the parents are not married and both wish to

be named on the birth certificate then both must attend at the registrar's office. Details of non-attendees cannot be entered.

A father who is not registered on the original birth certificate can be added later as re-registration is possible. However, this must be done with the mother's co-operation unless there is a court order based on a finding of his parentage.

Legalities of the name itself

In registering a birth you are stating the name by which it is intended that the child will be known. Unlike many countries, we have no rules about family names; an adult's name is that by which they are generally known and it is for parents to choose the surname by which

---

Not registering for political reasons

One potential drawback of not registering would seem to be needing to produce a birth certificate to get a passport. However, there can be advantages to not being registered at birth.

A Christian Anarchist Community in East Yorkshire called the Brotherhood Church has refused to recognise any state authority over its members since it started in the early 1900s. Consequently children born at the community were not registered. This resulted in at least one woman and her new born daughter serving a month's sentence in Armley gaol in 1916 and other parents being either fined or let off. However none of the children were ever put on the register, indicating that no-one but the parents of the child can register a birth. Due to lack of official registration one of the children born at the community failed to receive any call-up papers during World War II – very useful for a pacifist community. Also in more recent times members have been able to travel freely in western Europe despite the fact that they have no birth certificate.

---

their child is known. In the past it was said that this was an aspect of a father's common law guardianship, but it must now be a matter for which there is equal parental responsibilty.

Each parent is therefore free to make a choice and disputes can be decided by a court (by a specific issue or prohibition steps order) according to what is best for the child. The same applies to changes of name.

Problems are most likely to arise if the parents are separated or divorced and the parent who the child lives with adopts a new surname which they wish the child to share; or if the child goes into care and lives with a foster family for a long time. The 1989 Children's Act provides that, where there is a residence order or a care order in force, no person may cause a child to be known by a new surname without either the written consent of every person who has parental responsibilty or the leave of the court. (1989 Children's Act, sections 13(1)(a), 33(7)(a).

Parents and Guardians in Legal Terms

Married parents each have parental responsibility (a legal term) which continues automatically until their death. An unmarried father may also acquire parental responsibility as a result of a court order.

Any parent with parental responsibility may appoint another individual to be the child's guardian in the event of her/his death. This person is known as a "testamentary guardian". In the past the appointment could only be made by will but the 1989 Act now says simply that it should be made in writing, dated and signed by the person making the appointment. It is also possible to make a later appointment which revokes an earlier one.

Clearly it is important to discuss the appointment with a potential guardian and to get their agreement before naming him or her. If the person changes their mind later it is obviously best for all concerned if they let the parent know at the earliest opportunity so that a new guardian may be appointed. A person appointed guardian can disclaim their appointment, provided that they do so within a reasonable time.

Guardianship cannot take effect until all remaining persons with parental responsibility (usually both parents) have died. A guardian is expected to take full responsibility for the child's upbringing. S/he is treated like a parent for child welfare and protection purposes but does not have financial liability to other people, or to the state for the child's maintenance. Her/his criminal liability for neglect, ill-treatment or failure to educate is, however, the same as that of a parent. A guardian may themselves appoint a testamentary guardian to take their place in the event of their own death.

Issues to consider when choosing a name

This is a book about the potential ceremony that can be associated with naming, it is not a book about choosing a name – there are dozens of name-list publications and web sites available which can help you to select a name. However, it's inevitable that the utterance of the name itself will form a central focus of any naming ceremony and all sorts of images and thoughts will be triggered in people's minds when they hear what it is. A name can never be a mere tag. Whether it is unusual or commonplace it will always say something to people who hear it – to somehow express the spirit of the person. So in this section we're going to take a look at the (often hidden) processes that are going on when a name is chosen. Choosing a name is a design process and we usually have three clients (or groups of clients) that we are trying to satisfy:

Ourselves ... the namers

The name will say more about us than anybody else. It will say how much we want to conform and how much we want to be different. It will express the vision that we have for our child.

The named

Nowadays, thank goodness, parents do tend to think forward a bit and imagine how the chosen name may impact upon the life of their offspring – how will it sound shouted across a school playground, for instance? The curious thing is that the named never get a say in the process – but unless they rename themselves they are going to have to live with the result long after the namers are dead and buried!

The wider community ... the people around you

This may be people close to you and/or your extended family. How much are you trying to please these people? Watch out ... you may find that even if you think you're being outrageously different you may just be doing it to conform to the requirements of your peer group!

Here are the five main areas that we think you should consider when selecting a name for a child:

Feeling of ease with the name

Will we feel comfortable saying this name? Will the child feel comfortable? Will other people feel comfortable? Most people when asked why they have chosen a particular name just say something bland along the lines of: "We liked it". The slightly more honest will say: "We were comfortable with it". That's fine but it's important to step back a level and be sure that you know the reason(s) that you feel at ease with the name. Often it will be because unconsciously (and sometimes consciously) you're a member of some "club" and you want your offspring to have one of the officially acceptable names. That way you're membership is further enhanced and your child will feel welcome from an early age.

So if you're a sloane ranger (existing or aspiring) then you'll be looking at Polly, Rupert, Caroline, Henry, Sophie, Jamie, and Charlotte as potential names. These names aren't used exclusively by sloane rangers and, of course, names do migrate from one social group to another but it's interesting to observe how this has worked within Britain's class structure. Names only move in one direction – upper to lower and there may be attempts by the so-called "upper class" to hang on to a name by maintaining a more elaborate spelling – Deborah not Debra – or an obscure pronunciation – Rafe not Ralph. In the past the use of the mother's maiden name as middle name or incorporated to become a hyphenated family name also indicated class origins but this now also increasingly happens in alternative politically correct marriages (particularly in the USA) where both husband and wife change their family name to a new double-barrelled composite.

The "club" that you belong to may relate to your nationality or regional origin. So, for instance, if you're of Cornish descent you might choose Jowan, Pascoe or Gershom for a boy; or Delisent, Jellian or Tamsin for a girl. If you're planning a naming ceremony then the regional link may well provide you with all sorts of imagery and ancient practices to draw on.

If you're an alternative type then at one time you would have gone for names like Leaf, Sky, Fern or Willow. In the 1960s and 70s children who would be growing up in a new age were thought to deserve new names which expressed harmony with the natural environment. This was only a little better than 17th century puritans had done when they invented

THINK YOURSELF LUCKY - WAIT 'TIL YOU HEAR MINE

THAT'S THE TROUBLE WITH POST-MODERN PARENTS

for their children names like Fight-the-good-fight (the less onerous Faith, Hope and Charity survive to this day). In the 1600s the kids had fire and brimstone to discourage them from leaving their parents' club. But for Ocean and Sunchild it was just a matter of going to see a solicitor!

Interestingly this has led to a learning process and bohemians now tend towards abbreviations of slightly out of fashion names (eg Alfie; Rosie) when naming their children. In fact what's going on now is just like the cycles in ownership of parts of a city. Built for the wealthy; becomes slightly run-down as rich owners find new stamping grounds; houses divided into flats occupied by working class families; bohemians move in when property prices are at their lowest; upwardly mobile spot interesting things happening and snap up houses while they are cheap; gentrification process begins; working class and bohemians forced out as the wealthy move back in. On this basis we can expect to see Alfred back as a popular name amongst the smart set in about 2030!

The names of the moment for modern pagans are Taliesin and Morgana. Other Arthurian characters still seem a little too extreme. "Arthur" itself provides an interesting case study. One hundred years ago the Victorian revival of interest in the Arthurian legends was at its height and Arthur became a popular name for boys – their parents imagining that they would become courageous and chivalrous when they grew up. Well... all those little Arthurs did grow up and ultimately they became old men. Meanwhile, Arthur became less popular as a name and so the modern perception of an Arthur is of an old man with spectacles – serious, dull and proper. Even though interest in the Arthurian Mythos is on the rise again it is still difficult to make the mind think of "King Arthur" rather than "Uncle Arthur". Perhaps when all those Arthurs who were growing up in the first half of the 20th century have died out and we've been through a 20 or 30 year period with relatively few Arthurs around then the name will have been cleansed of its real world associations and can be reperceived as connected to myth and romance once again.

The Arthur example shows clearly how it's our collective first hand experience which causes a name to date. If a name remains fashionable then older owners will be perceived as younger than they really are!

The name pool in which all this takes place is like a living entity. There's some kind of Darwinian thing going on with the survival of the name depending on the fitness of its owners. If more than a certain proportion of Mabels are overweight then Mabel will be perceived as a label for an overweight woman and new parents will stop using it for fear that their offspring will grow to become like the label. Once this process has started it is self-fulfilling. No new girls are given the name and so no bright, young Mabels appear to affect the public perception and tip the scale the other way. Ultimately Mabel dies out as a name as its elderly owners die off – many of them will not have been overweight at all! The difference from the natural world, however, is that a name can never become extinct. Generations later Mabel can be reborn as a popular name even though it may have lain dormant, like a seed underground, for decades.

Adaptability

Something which enables a name to survive despite people's negative associations with it is adaptability – the possibility of the more upbeat "Art" or "Artie" can even make Arthur acceptable! So a second question to ask yourself when you choose a name is: does it have a range of abbreviations that convey different associations. If it does then the son or daughter that becomes uncomfortable with the full name has other options to choose from without having to formally change his/her name.

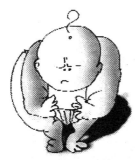

A NAME IS FOREVER

Microserfs
by Douglas
COUPLAND,
1995,
HarperCollins,
London

If a name can be adapted then you're giving your child a gift for which they may well be eternally grateful – a name that can be "freshened up" at a later stage. It's not that easy to predict how a name will evolve but if little James can become Jim, Jamie, Jimmy – or even Jam – according to his own taste then all the better.

The book *Microserfs* by Douglas Coupland gives us an idea which points to how quite ordinary names might be freshened up in the future. He suggests that we may not only use phonetic spelling in our language but also abbreviate so that if a letter is in upper case then it should be pronounced as its name (eg S = "es"); similarly with numbers (eg 2 = "too"). Other keyboard characters would also become available (eg @ = "at"). So if you want your offspring to have a name that will look cool on their e-mail address then consider some of the following: "k8" (Kate); "p@rik" (Patrick); "FE" (Effie); "Pt" (Pete); "LkE" (Elke); "MR" (Emma); "LEot" (Elliot); "RlEn" (Arlene); "m@" (Matt); "UGnia" (Eugenia); and don't forget "." (Dot)!

He also says that "@" may become the Mc or Mac of the new millennium. Extrapolating from this members of a family might then 'belong' to a ".fam" domain name in the way that they used to belong to a clan. So Ken McCarthy might become: kN@kRthE.fam

The ultimate adaptation can, of course, be gained with a unisex name. Interestingly, names which have ambiguous gender (eg Leslie, Lindsay, Robin, Vivian) have historically gone out of fashion quicker than others. This is thought to be because parents fear that these names will cause their sons to become effeminate and their daughters tomboys. Hopefully in the 21st century this will not be of such great concern and possibly even something to be encouraged!

Spelling, numbers of syllables, initials and rare letters

The mis-spelling and/or mispronunciation of one's name can be a lifelong source of irritation. Ponder well before you give your child a slightly different spelling of a well-known name (although it may well be worth it in the case of reclaiming an inheritance (eg using Gaelic spellings of Anglicised names like Sean for Shaun). An unusual name may also cause confusion with spelling (Is Crystal going to be Christel; Krystal; Christle etc etc?)

JUST CALL ME BUDDHA

It is said that you can't survive in showbiz if any of your names are longer than two syllables. School playground practice has always been to shorten names where possible and children with unshortenable, multi-syllabled names are often seen as being slightly weird/aloof/upper class. A modern exception to this would probably be Asian names which white anglo-saxon kids don't know how to abbreviate. As yet there has been negligible crossover of these names into mainstream British culture but when this does happen they will doubtless be subjected to the same pattern. When you're dreaming up first names consider how well they go with your family name. A first name with more syllables than the second name will often seem to end rather abruptly.

Initials too are important. Brian Alan Dodds – or B A D; Tara Isobel Totteridge – or ... When you put all the initials of your chosen name together do they add up to something that will make your son or daughter's schooldays hell? Pity the poor child whose mother gave birth on a Bakerloo Line train and decided to christen her offspring with the initials B A K E R L O O – yes it's a true story!

Any name which incorporates Q, X or Z (especially as an initial) will be more memorable. This works in a very subtle kind of way – look at Quentin, Xena and Zach, for instance. This may be something to think about when you consider ...

The uniqueness–ordinariness spectrum

Most people (particularly when they're young) want to be different but not so different that they will be made fun of. Generally parents want an established name for their child but one which is not too commonly used. There is an unspoken expectation that people with unusual names will have matching personalities and people with common names will be conformists.

There is something paradoxical in the fact that most people would express horror at the idea of the state allocating names to newborn babies (as if they were just mere identifying tags) and yet, given free choice, this is what an awful lot of parents do of their own accord! It's almost as if they're saying: "I name this child Susan. May she always keep her nose clean, blend into the crowd and not put her head above the parapet." Fortunately there are plenty of Susans who have proved that you don't have to grow up like your name!

In a global culture dominated by mass media a name can be reperceived and shift its position on the uniqueness/ordinariness spectrum overnight. In one generation Jason and Kylie have been transformed from rare names (drawn from Greek and Celtic origins) into commonplace names – and all thanks to a couple of Australian soap-opera stars.

Names most commonly given in the UK since 1925

Susan; Karen; Margaret; Sarah; Linda; Nicola; Carol; Claire; Catherine; and Tracy for girls.

David; John; Stephen; Paul; Michael; Andrew; Peter; Mark; Robert; and James for boys.

Of course the ultimate in uniqueness is to have an invented name. We've already seen that this didn't work very well for the Starchilds of this world but if the name is more abstract and sounds as if it could be a popular name in another culture then it can be effective. One method is to try and blend the parents' names. For instance Janet and Samuel decided to call their first child Jansam – it sounded vaguely Asian and Jansam, himself, liked it as he grew older. But there's a limit to how many ways that you can combine two names and Jansam's younger sister always felt that she wasn't as special in her parents' eyes as was her older brother.

Family traditions

Thank goodness we've at last grown out of the tradition of naming the first son after the father. Historically this had a lot do with the belief that the spirit of the parent would live on in the new child. This has been partly replaced by a more relaxed pattern of giving names of favourite relatives as second or third names. It can be nice also to give the opposite gender version of a parent or relative's name (naming Erica after her Uncle Eric).

But there can, of course, be other traditions within a family (see opposite) and important links can be made to these traditions in a naming ceremony. It has to be remembered that with each generation half the ancestry come from a new family and the new half may not necessarily approve of the tradition. It's hard work starting a new tradition, particularly in this day and age when everything changes so quickly and every generation strives to be different from its parents. If you're considering inventing a new naming tradition for your family then put yourself in the place of your grandchildren

Finn's Naming

I can't recall much about the naming ceremony for my son Finn, although I know we planted an apple tree in the orchard at Laurieston Hall, over the placenta. I've no idea what was said. But I see that choice as representing my belief in the unity of life forms, that the cyclical nature of life should be recognised, that as nature feeds us (the apple), so we should feed and care for nature (the placenta) – giving something back to replace that which we take. Also something about a commitment to place, to being rooted, though I haven't managed to live up to that one.

My belief system was also expressed in the lullaby I wrote for him:

I want you to sing before you can talk.
I want you to swim before you can walk.
And life seem like play, even the work.

More formally, I would say that I believe that each person is born with unique gifts, which the world needs, and that if you manage to fulfil those gifts, then your life will be full of joy. The fact that I sang it to him, and he can remember it, means that as a way of passing on my wishes and beliefs it was more effective than the naming ceremony itself, though how he interprets it, and/or lives it, is out of my hands.

And the name itself. I was following a tradition in my family, which recalls my Irish great grandmother, with names like Maeve and Fionnavar. I chose Finn after the traditional story of the lad helping a magician roast the salmon who has fed on the hazel nuts, and possesses great wisdom. Whoever has the first taste of the salmon will inherit the wisdom. The boy burns his finger, licks it, and so gets the wisdom, to the annoyance of the magician. So I suppose I wanted him to be fortunate and wise. He is not named after Finn MacCuil who seems to me to be obsessed with fighting.

Catriona Stamp

DON'T CALL ME NAPOLEON

or great grandchildren. What kind of tradition would be a delight to uphold and what would be a burden? In other words what would be sustainable. The essence of a tradition is that it becomes more powerful the longer it continues so if you're the person to initiate it then don't expect to see the fruits of your labours!

Hidden meaning

This is the feature that most baby-name books are strong on. Most names started their lives as ordinary nouns or adjectives in somebody's language somewhere. The baby-name books will usually tell you what those, now forgotten, meanings are. "Bonum nomen bonum omen" is a Roman Proverb which means "A good name is a good omen". If you were Roman you would presumably use a "good" literal noun or adjective from Latin when naming your child ... who would choose a bad one? But classical cultures also pioneered "onomancy", the art of divining character and predicting the future from personal names. This involved looking into even more ancient meanings; anagrams and numerology. This last science had its origins with Pythagoras. Numbers would be given to letters (typically: A, J, S =1; B, K, T = 2 etc) and the whole name "added up". All sorts of things were then read into the result according to the final result.

Another branch of onomancy analyses names according to initial letters and the balance of letters. So, for instance, "J" is thought to be a sign of fair-mindedness and a well-balanced outlook. The person might have a faculty of judgement which others value. A person whose "name-print" is dominated by J probably keeps a diary. They may also have a rather static quality about them so their total name-print needs more dynamic elements to help counteract this.

Your dreams and aspirations

There is always a danger that a person's name becomes a placard which says "this is where I came from and this is what the people that named me envisioned I would be like". Name choice is undoubtedly value-ridden. People say that they "like" a name when what they are really saying is that they like the associations that they have with the name. Try it yourself, would you call your son Adolf or Judas? But it's an impossible task to provide a name which will be totally appropriate in an unpredictable future so in many ways the name for the "dream future" is the only really honest one. Inevitably we look at what is around us (in our lives, books, films etc) for the name tag which is closest to our dream.

In this day and age any associations that you have with a name will, more than likely, be rubbished by your child when they grow up. There is always the danger, however, of it going the other way. The chosen name association can be too much of a challenge to the offspring, just too much to live up to. In Britain parents would scarcely consider naming their son Jesus – and yet, ironically, in Spain it's quite a common name.

The weird thing about your name is that the people who know you just chant it like a meaningless mantra. It's the people that you're meeting for the first time that it really has an impact on. It is all part of their first impression of you. Those hoping to become stars often adopt stage names – Peggy Hookham became Margot Fonteyn. A stage name or author's pseudonym have to be as carefully concocted as any corporate identity. In an increasingly image conscious world perhaps we should all have a number of aliases that could be used in different contexts. The people that do this already are loving couples witrh their pet names like Angel Chops and Dazzlebum. In Mongolia these names are more public ... so Muhai, said in the right context, means 'Darling' as well as 'Ugly' and nobody minds having the name Sazug (Smelly) because it means that he smells quite nice!

On carrying an unnamed child

Within days of announcing to my family that I was pregnant I was being asked whether I wanted a boy or a girl and what name I would give it. I was surprised that anyone could be thinking so far ahead. As far as I was concerned even the word 'baby' belonged to the future, all I was carrying was energy. Consequently, when I started thinking about a name for our unborn child, I felt as though I was imposing an identity and a future onto something that has no awareness of society as yet. It feels like naming changes the rhythm of a thing, gives it edges and defines it as a separate entity. I was told that in some cultures, mothers hold their babies until the child is ready to separate itself from its mother. The baby wants to participate in its mother's life, not to be entertained by objects with no warmth or heartbeat. I wondered whether giving a name soon after birth was a way of creating separation between mother and child. Perhaps naming could occur when the baby is ready to enter the world of language and meaning. Could we call it 'our baby' till a name suggests itself?

Friends who plan to have children have sometimes talked to me about names they like. They guard them so that once told there is no way you could steal that name for your own. The names are often chosen from a position they take in the world. "I wouldn't call it X, that's far too trendy."/"I only like Irish names for boys." I would never give a child a name that reminded me of someone I dislike. Inherent in this is the sense that names evoke characteristics or qualities that we would like or not like our children to have. Some names feel tragic, superficial, ordinary, or sacrificial because of associations with people you've known or fictional characters you've read about. In late 1997, I wonder how many couples would have called their daughters Diana, and I am pretty sure there must have been a drop in boys named Charles. Before we committed ourselves to having a child, it felt quite romantic to discuss names we might choose. It was also a way of finding out whether we had the same taste. As it turned out the discussions were more like:

"You wouldn't would you?"
"Why, what's wrong with that name?"
"He'll get teased at school"

"Rubbish! If you're going to get teased you get teased, it's got nothing to do with the name."

"Well, I am sure he won't thank you!"

"It's a strong name, he'll stand out from all the other children."

"A strong name doesn't mean the child will have a strong character."

... and so on.

What it revealed was that not only were we trying to anticipate the identity of the child but also the situations that the child might have to confront. A mixture of parental responsibility in wanting to get it right for the child and self-preservation in wanting to avoid pain for ourselves.

I know a few couples who have chosen a fairly rare first name followed by a more ordinary middle name, so the child can change it if they want to. In a few cases friends' children have changed their name when they left home to go to university for instance. The opportunity to start fresh amongst new people allows them to consider creating a new identity. A good idea if you've always hated your name and felt that it prevented you from being the person you saw yourself as. You can't change your height, but you can change your name.

So where does all this leave me? Two months pregnant, I am having my first scan next week. When I'm staring at the screen and see a tiny, tiny formless thing, will a name like Joanna come to mind? It didn't occur to me, until I talked about this with a friend who had her children before scans were available, that I might choose not to look at the image. It could be interpreted as the first act of separation, the foetus is perceived outside of my body. How timely that I should be thinking about these issues now. Once that image is in my head I can never go back to the place I am in as I write, where my image is a mixture of sensations and rhythms rather than shape and lines. Whether I choose to look or not, at least I have had a chance to reflect and think about what this process means to me and what my relationship to the technology will be.

Tanya Peixoto

YOUR CHILDREN ARE NOT YOUR CHILDREN

Your children are not your children.

They are the sons and daughters of Life's longing for itself.

They come through you but not from you,

And though they are with you yet they belong not to you.

You may give them your love but not your thoughts,

For they have their own thoughts.

You may house their bodies but not their souls,

For their souls dwell in the house of to-morrow, which you cannot visit, not even in your dreams.

You may strive to be like them, but seek not to make them like you.

For life goes not backward nor tarries with yesterday.

You are the bows from which your children as living arrows are sent forth.

extract from "On Children"
by Kahlil Gibran

PART FOUR
IMPROVEMENTS AND
ALTERNATIVES

There *are* ways of making the processes of welcoming a new person into the world both better and more meaningful for all concerned. In this section we look at the broader context: from improving the place where the baby is actually born to dealing with the wider issues of family ownership. We also show how a naming ceremony can be the start of something which carries on throughout an individual's life – whether it is by making links to later birthdays and celebrations or by initiating the support structure which Godparents (or whatever you choose to call them) will provide.

Improvements around Family Dynamics

A new person arriving in a family will not only affect the status quo amongst existing children but will also, invariably, create expectations amongst older relatives. If you decide to put together your own naming rite then you may like to consider some of the issues that are raised and think of how you might design the ceremony so that it can symbolically include those who may feel excluded; as well as pre-empting objections from those who would prefer something more traditional.

Dealing with Family Ownership

You announce you are pregnant. Suddenly, it's not safe for you to eat certain foods, travel on buses, go on

Place of Birth: Getting what is right for you

The atmosphere of a place can make all the difference between feeling relaxed and at ease with yourself or being tense and anxious. We often prepare a place for a special occasion like decorating a room for a birthday party or a wedding. We clear the decks before starting work, we all need a personal place in our homes where we express ourselves, a notice board or fridge. The way we decorate, the colours we use, is of great importance to most of us. So why do we accept the institutional egg-shell blue walls of a hospital room, not a picture in sight, a view of the road, and the smell of detergent when we're about to give birth? Surely it must be one of the most sacred acts there are. Why aren't there special birthing temples or units that don't cost a fortune? Where mothers are pampered and valued and babies are welcomed as spiritual beings. So perhaps I'm just fussy and indulgent but why don't we start by giving our babies the best there is. The best is available but at a price. I recently got a brochure about a birthing unit that made me actually look forward to the birth. It promised quality care, 24 hour helpline, accommodation for you and your partner, a choice of menu, top midwives and consultants, waterbirths, aromatherapy, massage and so on. My local hospital with its huge incinerator and sixties architecture, its grey sprawling buildings that go on and on just doesn't inspire me. I want to campaign for places that reflect the importance, the delicacy and freshness of a being's first breath. Perhaps if money were to be allocated to improving the experience of giving birth then it would start to look as though we really were committed to our children and their futures.

Tanya Peixoto

holiday; you are carrying a very precious commodity: A grandchild, a niece, a daughter, not only does it connect you with your own family but also your partner's family as well. You and your baby belong. Of course that can feel wonderful. It can also feel overwhelming. There may not have been a baby in your family for many years. If it's the first grandchild or great grandchild,

Getting what is right for you within the NHS

A woman does not need to have her baby at home or to pay for an independent midwife in order to have care that is suited to her individual needs. At the Rural Maternity Unit in Penrith, Cumbria we believe that it can be obtained within the NHS. Women and their partners are encouraged to question the facilities on offer and the philosophy of their carers. It is only by complete openness that they can decide what is right for them. From the first contact with her midwife in early pregnancy a woman is made to feel that no question is too trivial or any request taboo.

A woman with a low risk pregnancy can choose to have her baby at our midwife/GP unit at Penrith, at the Obstetric unit at Carlisle, 20 miles away, or at home. At Penrith the birth rooms are wallpapered, have pictures and there is a distant view of trees and hills. The bed is at the side of the room to enable the woman to use a greater area of floor space, to walk, kneel, sit or do whatever gives her most comfort. A radio, cassette and disc player is available for any music of her choice, which can be anything from Bach to Hendrix. The midwives encourage active labour and birth because of the benefits to mother and baby but this is not wanted by every woman, and we respect their wishes. In recent years all the midwives have had to build up their knowledge of complementary therapies in order to support women who wish to use them. There are also midwives who are homeopaths who can be consulted by the woman and a midwife who is a reflexologist.

The saying "You only get one chance to make a first impression" can not be more true than with birth. A never to be forgotten experience. At Penrith we believe that we have a duty to make it a truly precious and unique moment.

Ann West – an NHS midwife

everyone will seem to have an investment and although the attention may be nice for a while, it may start to feel to the mother as if she is losing her identity; everyone has so much advice to give her. Your life does change because your family suddenly has a fantastic excuse to come visiting, whether you like it or not. How do you deal with this? The obvious way is to be firm and assertive about how you want to do things, if you can be. Perhaps becoming a mother is a rite of passage in itself, an opportunity to change the nature of your relationship to the rest of the family. One mother felt that if she tried to please all the members of her family who showed a passionate interest in seeing her daughter, then she would have been constantly away from home. That could have been enjoyable except that it was a time at which she wanted to be at home!

When people start to see your baby, they immediately look for family resemblances. "Doesn't she look like her father?" As the baby grows, and starts to assert its personality it becomes, "She's quite a character, reminds me of her grandmother". There is a form of family ownership going on here which can result in labels that stick. Some forms of projection for instance, she's very academic like her aunt, whilst he's more artistic like his uncle, are fine if the role models are positive, but if they are not then children can spend years trying to prove that they are not artistic, because they don't want to be compared with their uncle.

There is a distinction between being owned and belonging. In its most extreme form where perhaps religion and culture prevent people from being themselves each individual has to decide whether rejecting the family is worth it or not. For most of us, where families can be a little too demanding, it takes negotiation and accepting that sometimes we have to say no. You must put your needs and those of your baby first and let everyone else sort themselves out.

Beware the Focus on the Latest Child

Each parent will deal with this in their own way. However, sometimes important things go unsaid and children often need you to start a conversation with them in order to express what they really feel. It may be that they are worried they might have to share their room, toys or deeper still, their parent's love and attention. It's worth talking about these things before the baby is born. It may be helpful to emphasise to older siblings that the love you have for the family is not finite ... with each person's allocation getting less as the family grows. A friend described a ritual she and her eldest son had which involved allocating "Our time" without the baby. Every day after school, she managed to spend some time with him alone.

Children have a strong sense of fairness. If one can achieve a sense of balance, the child feels they can trust you. The "I always get blamed for everything" can be a difficult one to deal with. How does the older children feel to see presents and cards arriving for the baby, or even "their" pram, cot, clothes being used again? Each child reacts differently, but some children are very attached to their objects and it can be very painful. One way of dealing with this is to ask the eldest child permission to use her/his things and be prepared not to if s/he says no. The other is to draw on their knowledge and expertise of which particular toys, clothes etc are useful and fun to play with.

Women who have just had babies themselves will know that it is the mother who feels tired and touchy and in need of attention. It is hard not to be entirely consumed by the baby that has been physically part of you for the last nine months. Perhaps some friends and relatives are sensitive enough to realise that the eldest child may be feeling a bit left out and make a fuss of him/her without over-doing it and giving the child the feeling that everyone has gone completely mad!

Acknowledging and Including children from other relationships

It helps if you like children and enjoy talking and playing with them. Some people only like their own children and that is how it is for them. If you remember what it felt like to be rejected as a child you may well, as far as possible, try to include and acknowledge any children from other relationships that are members of your family. However difficult the circumstances are, the children need to be loved, accepted and not made responsible for their parents' actions. Here are some ways of showing that you care:

- Listening and taking their feelings seriously, asking their opinion, eg on decorating the house

- Having an independent view on things

- Spending time with them on their own and also allowing them space with their own parent

- Giving presents and remembering their birthdays

- Inviting them to family get-togethers.

- Photos of them around the house and in albums

- Discussing how they would like to be referred to, eg my half-sister or just my sister

JUST LOOK AT THEM - WHEN WILL THEY GET THE HANG OF THIS PARENTING THING?

- Acknowledging and praising their parents

- Going on day trips and holidays together.

My step-son lives with his mother and comes to us for weekends. I felt a need to acknowledge how he might feel about me being pregnant and in the process I realised just how much I love and appreciate him.

A letter to my Step-son

Nearly nine years ago I blasted into your dad's life, I've come to stay I silently promised you, too many women before me, I know the scene, my father was a bit the same. And in the end you've got to worry about his loneliness, I'll do some of the things that make it feel like home, like Sunday dinner and planting bulbs, you let me in, you let me learn.

You didn't criticise when I got it wrong, though I kept waiting for you to say, "Enough, I want her out of here!" But you didn't, you let me stay. And when I asked you if I could rent part of your room, to do my work and make my books, you thought about it and then said yes, which gave me space, the space I need.

And when we said we're getting married, you said "'bout time" and laughed and joked. You were best man, "It's good dad's got Tanya but Tanya's lucky to have dad too".

Now I'm asking you after 18 years to share it all again. A baby's on its way. I know how I felt when my dad said the same to me. A half-brother or sister and a step-mother and father. No half love or step love. No change in how we feel. You are our one and only Jake.

Though the house is crammed with junk and there isn't space for more I promise you won't have to share, there'll always be a place for you.

This is really to say thank you, I'm just so proud of our relationship and amazed by your consistency, your warmth and generosity.

Tanya

Sometimes your 'own' child may feel a little resentful of the attention you give to other children, especially if s/he doesn't receive the same from the equivalent 'other' adult. Discuss this with your step-child. However difficult it is for them to understand you have to trust that they will eventually.

More complex situations occur when there is acrimony in a couple's relationship. The father, for instance, may want nothing to do with the child but his parents react quite differently. They are excited about the birth of a grandchild and feel a bond with the new baby. We know of a situation where the christening took place and the grandparents were invited and went – despite the fact that their son didn't want them to go. They are determined that this child should know her family even if she doesn't know her father. One can appreciate what they are trying to do and at the same time recognise how difficult it is for all concerned.

Improvements around Spiritual Parenting

This new person will not always be a cute little baby in a christening robe and it is important to acknowledge this by creating features of the naming ceremony which will reach out into her or his life. Gilly Adams tells us of her experience of being a Godparent:

How do you choose Godparents?

With the loss of meaning from conventional christenings and the absence of ceremonies to replace them, godparenting can often become a kind of social activity; the sort of thing that parents might bestow as an honour on friends or family, without a clear understanding of the significance of the role or the

Taking the God out of God-parent:
Finding a different word

If you're not a Christian and you're not planning a traditional christening then you'll probably want to find an alternative to the word **Godparent**. But you'll notice that we've stuck with it in this book ... partly because most people understand, more-or-less, what it means. However, as we point out on page 65, a formal Godparent does make a very specific vow.

Guardian has the right connotations but it does have a meaning in Law.

Mentor is good but people may feel uncomfortable describing themselves with the word. "I'm little Freddy's mentor" – try saying it yourself! Mentor has also been purloined by the world of National Vocational Qualifications so may well become debased over the next few years!

Spiritual Parent is accurate if you want the spirit but not the specific god. But it's a bit of a mouthful.

Supporting Adult says that right thing but has some of the wrong associations.

The most accurate word that we've seen (for what most people want) is **Lay-parent** – it implies a person who will act in some kind of parental role but who is not the "professional" parent.

Perhaps, as you make your choice you should mull over this quotation on the difference between parents and mentors ...

"As caretakers, parents cannot also be mentors. The roles and duties differ. It is enough for a parent to keep a roof over your head and food on the table, and to get you up and off to school. Providing a cave of security, a place for regressions is no small job. Freed of these tasks, the mentor has only one: to recognise the invisible load you carry and to have a fantasy about it that corresponds with the image in the heart. One of the most painful errors we make is to expect from a parent a mentor's vision and blessing and strict teaching, or expecting from a mentor shelter and concern for our human life."

from **The Soul's Code - In Search of Character and Calling**
by James Hillman, Random House, New York, 1996

responsibilities which might be involved. It's likely that the potential godparent shares this lack of clarity and may not be envisaging much more than a promise to send cards and presents for Christmas and birthdays. And yet, with the breakdown of so many marriages and the frequent absence of the traditional extended family, godparenting presents a real opportunity to bring other adults into a child's life, people who may have the potential to enrich the child spiritually as well as materially. Although godparent is the traditional title for this role, it may be helpful to remove the "god" in order to open up the idea of what this person can do and offer, perhaps thinking of the fairy godmothers familiar to us from our childhood, who were able to offer magic gifts at moments of importance or need in a child's life.

For the parents the need to "appoint" godparents provides the opportunity to look amongst your family and friends to find the person(s) whom you would like to be significant figures in your child's life, or, in other words, the people with whom you would like to share your child. You are probably looking for someone who will take a regular interest in the child's life and be capable of being a genuine alternative parent at times of need. Or perhaps you can consider what gifts you would like for your child – humour, compassion, fun, creativity, eccentricity, time – and think of someone who has these qualities and will be able to provide the child with experiences which may be different from those on offer within the family. Another possibility is linking the godparent role with that of legal guardian, so that this person would also be someone who would make a commitment to look after the child should something happen to you. Unlike godparenting, which has no legal status, you need to identify the person who has agreed to be a guardian in your will so that s/he has the status to adopt this role should the need arise. If you are uncomfortable with godparent as a title, you may want to find another term which more accurately describes the person's special qualities and role.

Returning the Favour

A childless couple who were friends of my parents became, respectively, Godmother to my sister and Godfather to me. They were fairly low-key Godparents and, much to our relief, didn't push the Christianity beyond giving us both Bibles! My Godfather died some years ago but his widow lives on and is now in her late nineties. She lived on her own and a relative (who, himself, was in his 70s) kept an eye on her. Then he died! A couple of years later my sister suggested that she might move in with her and her family. Initially she was reluctant to take up the offer feeling that she didn't want to be a burden. Eventually death and relocation of near neighbours in the street (where she had lived for 50 years) left her very isolated and she decided to take the plunge. Her house was sold and some of the money used to pay for an extension to my sister's home. At the age of 94 she was suddenly thrown into a completely new environment with two working adults, two moody teenagers, computers, mobile phones and all the other paraphernalia of modern life. She loves it and it has given her a whole new lease of life. It's now very difficult to believe that she was born in 1904 when you see her on a Saturday night outing to the local Chinese retaurant! In a funny sort of way this "Godchild caring for aged Godparent" relationship can work better than the more traditional "child caring for aged parent" set-up – the reason being, presumably, that the various parties don't bring as much emotional baggage to the situation!

Jonathan How

If you are being asked to be a godparent, don't accept without thinking carefully about what this will mean. To work properly, it should be a commitment which extends beyond the day of the christening or naming ceremony. Do you feel drawn to this particular child? How much time and energy can you offer? Is it likely that you could keep up a relationship with him or her over a period of years? Are you likely to go on knowing and being friendly with the child's parents? If not, will you still be able to be there for the child? It is also helpful to ask what you want yourself from the relationship? If you've got children of your own, what place will this child have? If you are childless, how will you accommodate this child or children in your life? It is also worth remembering that eventually this will become a two way relationship. That loveable baby will become a person and you may or may not like each other. Certainly, like any other relationship, this bond will require maintenance and work, and you may need some ground rules. Do you want to keep things light or will you be prepared to cope with the bad times and the occasional need to say difficult things? Are you taking on the idea of spiritual parenting in any way, with the implication that this will involve you in sharing your values and your perspective of the world?

Creative godparenting is not something to be assumed lightly. It is an enormous privilege to be given access to a special relationship with a child in this way, a relationship which can bear witness to the uniqueness of that child and offer a different perspective on the perplexing maze of family relationships. Done properly there will inevitably be times when it seems a burden but this is a commitment which also carries the potential for love and fun and a great deal of mutual enrichment.

Can you acquire Godparents later?

What do you do if you didn't get any Godparents? Do you feel like you missed out? Do you need one right now? Maybe you would rather have Guardians, Lay-parents or a Mentor …

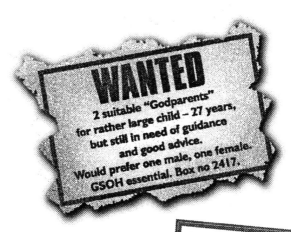

WANTED

2 suitable "Godparents" for rather large child – 27 years, but still in need of guidance and good advice. Would prefer one male, one female. GSOH essential. Box no 2417.

Dear Beryl

You've known me all of my life, so you're used to my strange ideas by now. I realised today that although I'm technically a 'grown up' (27.5!) I seem more and more in need of advice. You are full of wise words and handy hints. Would you become my belated Godmother Beryl? It would mean so much if you did. Think it over. We'll speak soon.

Love Hannah XXX

If belated Lay-parents transpire as a result of your attempts then you may need to create a suitable 'bonding' ceremony between you.

Hannah Fox

Guardianship and Godparenting

I am a woman without biological children. The knowledge that that would be so has been with me since I was young and, at different times, the grief of that knowledge has impacted on my whole life. It has felt like a failure of my femaleness and an emptiness at the centre of my being – a vacancy in the meaning of my life.

There was a time when this loss threatened to overwhelm me and to defend myself against it, I defended myself against other people's children with the excuse that I had none of the requisite experience to deal with them. Then, some things changed for me: in a discussion that was nothing to do with me personally a colleague remarked with conviction that biological motherhood had nothing to do with the capacity to mother. Not unconnected, but some time later, I began to have the confidence to explore the possibilities in my relationships as a Godmother, as a positive alternative to full-time motherhood.

I have acquired my Godchildren in different ways: first came three brothers who are the sons of friends I met twenty-six years ago in my first professional job. Knowing that I was unlikely to have children of my own, they offered me a share in their first-born son and then decided to consolidate my role by attaching me to the other boys when they subsequently appeared. Two other Godchildren have come through different parts of my family – my middle brother's son and my eldest brother's daughter – and these were less considered, more conventional invitations which coupled being an aunt with the particular role of Godmother. Finally, there is the daughter of a dear friend, who is fifteen years younger than me. This was a specific brief: to be a significant other adult in this child's life, someone to whom she could turn and with whom she would feel comfortable and at home, someone who would be there for her and who would provide a sense of extended family.

I am not a believer in organised religion, although I have come to have a strong sense of things spiritual as I have got older, so the experience of making the Godparent's vows in the various churches involved, has been a strange one. I negotiated with the parents in advance about what my commitment would be and concentrated on this whilst listening to the words of the service. I haven't been able to promise in my heart to bring someone up as a Christian, but I have been able to promise some kind of loving and caring. For all those children I have accepted, in addition, the responsibility of being a legal Guardian in the event of something happening to their parents – as a separate but somehow interwoven commitment. For my last Goddaughter, no church naming was involved, and I had a detailed agreement with her mother about what I was being asked to do and what I could offer.

When the child is small, the process is easy. Presents for birthdays and Christmas, occasional letters and cards and visits as permitted by geography. As the child grows the relationship must become two-way or it will wither and disappear. After all, like their blood parents, I have been imposed on these children, but less inescapably, so we could decide that we don't suit each other and let the relationship dwindle (my own Godparents have played no significant part in my life).

The change came for me when I realised that I could use the gift of my Godchildren as a way of being actively involved with younger people in my life, rather than mourning my own childlessness. I took this on as a renewed commitment in my life and one into which I would have to invest time and energy, and run the risk of rebuttal too. When my oldest Godson was at university, I wrote and asked what he wanted from me as a Godmother, pointing out that, unfortunately, I had very little money so couldn't offer significant gifts. He responded warmly and it's become clear that we do have things to share with each other like a mutual interest in the arts and a perspective on his family life (which has suddenly become important since his parents have split up recently). It's made me realise that I would love – even now – to have someone in my life who has known me and my family over the years and could bear witness to what has gone on. With my younger Godchildren I am concentrating on my potential as a "fairy" Godmother, purveyor of treats and outings, inventor of rituals, familiar enough to trust but not omnipresent like a parent. I haven't yet found a way to connect with two of them – and perhaps I never will – but I hope that nevertheless I can offer a sound enough presence to be approached in time of trouble.

For me being a Godmother has become a source of riches. It seems to me a useful role which could be tailor-made for each relationship. What's needed, however, is a new title which would be less restrictive and more indicative of the value of this relationship in everyday life.

Gilly Adams

Improvements around the Ceremony

Deciding what <u>you</u> want

The birth of a child is (usually) an occasion for enormous joy. However shy we are about expressing ourselves, for most of us the gift of life is a miracle which taps into our deepest emotions, and the desire to celebrate that miracle is archetypal. Given such profound feelings, it is not surprising that it may be difficult to find a ceremony which will convey exactly what we want to say. The Christian baptism service is the traditional way of announcing and celebrating the birth of a child to our friends and families, and also of making our commitments to that child public, but for non Church-goers it may not be the most appropriate ceremony ... although it *will* be the most available one. If you want to celebrate the arrival of your child you could start by thinking about what exactly it is that you want to say and what will be the best forum for saying it. If you want your child christened in church but don't know exactly what that involves, you can find a copy of the service in the library or in a bookshop so that you can see what words will be used and whether they feel right to you. You can also make an appointment to see the Vicar and ask any questions you may have about what will happen, how many children will be christened at the same time etc, so that you can gather enough information to decide whether this ceremony is appropriate for you or whether you need to be bold and create an alternative occasion more in keeping with your own lifestyle and beliefs. Accepting the church service because it is traditional and available, and what older relatives will expect, may result in disappointment instead of celebration and you may find that a song and a poem in the middle of a party in the garden would make you happier. The important thing is to think carefully in advance about what exactly you want and then go out to create exactly that.

Baby Naming Ceremonies: something more personal

Your baby has arrived safely, you've chosen the name, and you want a ceremony to celebrate this, with friends and family, which give them an opportunity to greet the new arrival. You want to state in front of them your commitments to the unconditional love and care, support and encouragement, respect and responsibility you will continue to provide as a parent.

By expressing your choices, about when, where, who and what, you will create a ceremony that is personal and unique to this occasion. A naming on a beach at dawn on a summer's morning will be very different from a gathering around a log fire in someone's home on a winter's afternoon. Decisions should not be made for the sake of being different. It is best to reflect on what setting feels right. Some people love the outdoors and may include a short walk through a favourite landscape, to the spot for the naming, but for others the most important factor may be to ensure that a certain member of the family with health or mobility problems is able to attend, and they will therefore select a place, possibly indoors, to make that possible.

The time of year as well as the time of day will colour the form of the ceremony, if you take on board what it allows you to use on the day

The Naming of Dorian Boyd

born at the winter equinox 1977
named near the summer
equinox 1978

SEQUENCE

Procession
Making and
Lighting the
Space
Stories
Song
Speech
Naming
Celebration &
Presents

As the wind ties skeins
In the heart of a tree
So the wind blows seeds
in the air

As the wind folds petals
in the lattice of bone
So the wind blows men
to the stars

As the wind drives smoke
to the edge of a field
So the wind finds fire
in the sky.

Then the eagle soared above my head and
fluttered there and suddenly the sky was full
of friendly wings all coming toward me. Black Elk

– snow? autumn berries for decoration? candles? strawberries and cream? kites?

The presence of several other young children means you need to include something for them – a quest? a treasure hunt? gifts or tasks on the day?

Baby Naming Society

Baby Naming Society

Founded in 1995 (as the Family Covenant Association) by Lord Young of Dartington, the Baby Naming Society offers help, support and inspiration to parents seeking an alternative to church baptisms.

They advise on a naming ceremony to suit personal circumstances and they will prepare a personalised script for the occasion. They can help find a celebrant to lead it. The core of their ceremony is an invitation to the new parents to make a commitment to care for their child's upbringing. The BNS feels that when this expresses intentions that they have thought through together, they are more likely to be kept.

The main resource available is a guide with background information on the significance of namings, advice on organising the venue and the day, inspirational poems and readings, plus a section on legal matters between parents and their child.

A special certificate will be supplied for signing on the day. Preparation takes three weeks and the fees are very modest.

By 1998 Lord Young was wanting to make these ceremonies more mainstream by suggesting that registrars lead them. This would require a change in the law.

Church baptisms have declined in number – now only one in four babies is baptised.

See Part Five for the address of the Baby Naming Society.

In Part Five you will find suggestions for words and music to use and ideas for mementos of the day. At the end of Part Four you can read about other people's naming ceremonies.

Do what these families did. Work to your strengths. If the baby's new aunt or uncle is a talented musician, find a way of involving them in the ceremony. if your neighbour produces abundant plants, herbs or flowers, get them involved in decorating the space. A calligrapher friend, or desk-top publishing enthusiast could make you special invitations or certificates. A colleague who loves model making might create a special gift or centrepiece.

Keep it simple so that you, if you are new parents, do not get too exhausted to enjoy it. Friends love to be asked to take on a job, so delegate. Make it clear that this is their gift to you – organising the transport, mowing the lawn in readiness, overseeing catering on the day, or co-ordinating accommodation for visitors.

Just by holding a naming ceremony, you express the importance of the occasion as your child takes its place in its community. By taking the time and trouble to create a special ceremony, you are already conveying how committed a parent you are.

Understanding and Planning

Before we can write the ceremony we need first to look at and acknowledge who we are in terms of race, culture, religion and nationality. Information about the family group needs to be taken into account. Is this a first child or are there brothers and sisters? They need a role in the ceremony. Is the child in good health or otherwise? Even circumstances around the conception may be significant if this child was long awaited (see poem on page 20) or if there had been previous loss or sadness in the family. A naming for an adopted child needs to mark this special relationship.

Family politics may be straightforward, or complex in the event of a second family. Are there grandparents and will they be present? Any godparents or lay parents or guardians and if so what is their role?

If you are naming an infant, their input will be relatively passive and the ceremony will be an expression of the parents' values, wishes and declarations towards the child, plus, of course, an announcement of the chosen name. An older child being named – say eight years and upwards – will need and want a considerable input into the planning of the ceremony. Therefore, a process of collaboration, consultation and possibly compromise with the parent(s) will be appropriate, to look at their views and wishes around the naming, who and what it should involve ... starting with their consent.

When it is not a traditional baptism, it is most important to allow enough time beforehand to discuss the reasons for and the meaning of the ceremony with: the rest of the family, potential lay parents and in particular the grandparents, who may have very strong expectations, even if they are unstated.

The best way to ensure that the ceremony goes off without confusion or embarrassment, is to plan it very carefully and to leave plenty of time to draw up and write out any declarations; to practice; ideally to visit the site with all key participants (particularly if it is unfamiliar); and have a walk through.

Helping doubting family members to understand

If you decide to create your own naming ceremony, make it a priority to find the time to talk to the rest of your family. The majority of new grandparents will expect some sort of church baptism if there is to be a ceremony at all.

You will need to talk through clearly with them what meaning your ceremony has for you, why you want to do it, what it will entail and why you would value them being part of it. Only then may they begin to understand why you have chosen an alternative to the traditional christening service. They will need to feel comfortable about it, and confident that it is a "proper" event (with moments that are solemn and slightly formal), then they will feel positive about wanting to be part of it.

Neglecting this preparation may not spoil the actual day, but can store up disappointments and differences for the future. Older relatives can look on baptism as something of a spiritual insurance policy, even in non-churchgoing families. "Just in case anything should happen ... heaven forbid" are the unspoken fears.

Differences of religious practice can be accommodated. It is possible to carry out your ceremony and make space for a relative to add their prayer or blessing, and not compromise your own integrity. Why not call for a few moments of silent reflection which allows people space for their own prayers. Beware being too controlling.

Examples of Naming Ceremonies

Welfare State International has been involved in many naming ceremonies in its 30 year existence. Some of them are described on the following pages.

Naming of Ewan Philip Mahony

Chris and I had decided several months before Ewan was born that we wanted to mark his arrival in a special way. Christening was not an option for us because we are not Christians and have no wish to be hypocritical. But we certainly did not want the occasion to slip by without celebration.

We had read of naming ceremonies in **Engineers of the Imagination**. Chris had also seen a reference to the British Humanist Association in a Sunday newspaper and bought **New Arrivals** – their guide to naming ceremonies.

One of our first decisions was that we wanted the ceremony to be out of doors. Some of our greatest pleasures come from activities such as hill walking and orienteering. Indeed we met through orienteering. So we wanted to introduce Ewan to these delights early!

At first, getting to our preferred site was seen as an obstacle. Only gradually did we realise that the walk/journey could be a part of the ceremony and a metaphor to boot.

Another factor in choosing a site was that Chris's mum was seriously ill and we wanted a venue that she could easily reach by vehicle if necessary. In the end, sadly she was too ill to make it to the ceremony and died shortly afterwards. However she and Chris's dad sent a poem and she was able to enjoy the video and photographs we had taken.

Our first choice was a knoll at a local country sports estate with a wonderful panoramic view over Morecambe Bay and a sweep of hills leading up into the Lake District.

We had already started planning around this when we decided to ask Sue Gill and John Fox for some advice. John quite rightly cautioned against going much further before sounding out the estate. As he pointed out, the place informs the shape of the ceremony.

As luck would have it the agent for the estate was very suspicious of anything which wasn't clay pigeon shooting or fishing. Chris was heavily pregnant, but when we arrived at the agent's cottage she kept us standing out in the rain whilst she verbally doused more cold water on our ideas.

After this reverse we scoured local maps for alternatives. We had more or less settled on a hillside near us when, on a walk with my father, Chris suddenly beckoned us to the top of a small hill and said, "This is it". It was less spectacular than our first choice but had a good feel to it with its grotesquely wind-bent trees, limestone pavement and strangely cropped bushes.

Naming Ewan Philip

Ewan.

Soon, as you journey upon the earth,
your knowledge will widen.

Soon, the millennium will descend.
(When you will be all of five.)

Then,
too soon
as a young man, you will tread
along the seams.
On the lumpy patchwork edge
of our jewelled planet earth
you will voyage.
An adolescent continent
burning with volcanic youth.

Today we give you strength
before you go forth to the
hauntings
and the dauntings
of the waywardness of us.

Take strength upon this common
from the kinship that we offer.
Take our love and sustenance
from these roots on Urswick
Crags.

See the elm that's layerered,
with the skill and sweat of craft.
Sense the Bronze age settlement
where ancient people laughed.

On the Hoad at Ulverston,
the lighthouse is asleep.
While upon the moor behind
the talking masts all bleep.

Over there the sea,
still a saucer of mystery.
Here criss-cross of clint and grike
nurse sycamore and ash.

Each ounce of soil contains
a million living things.
Though each stile of rugged stone
permits just one to pass.

Here.
Ewan Philip
you are named.

Bursting your seams
To dance to your daddy
and your mammy
and your friends.

In this occasioning community,
between the limestone crags
and the craggy stars above.

May you take root.
Then fly.

And trampoline so high
from these crossing
threads of love.

These crossing threads of love.

John Fox

Initially Sue and John had encouraged us to look among our friends for someone to lead the ceremony. Having drawn a blank, we asked Sue, who we knew would be confident, informal and put people at their ease.

The next step was to walk the route together with Sue and John. Even on a mildish May evening it became obvious that somewhere a bit more sheltered was preferable. We carried on to a lower outcrop studded with trees, which also had a strongly individual character but was more enclosed. It also had the advantage of being much closer to a road. Guests whose toddlers could not manage the walk could take this short cut and gear could be brought in by van.

We were apprehensive that the many young bullocks on the land might worry people, so we asked one of our guests, who happens to be a farmer, if he would keep an eye on this. What we didn't expect was that they would try to eat all our bunting, knocking down all the poles, etc. Ella, our "stage manager" had to mount guard to prevent a re-occurence.

Far from the cattle frightening our guests, the kids loved trying to stroke their noses. They also provided a photogenic backcloth as they gathered round at a respectful distance.

We agonised about how to involve our relatives in the ceremony and ditched many ideas as we tried to get the right balance of ritual, poetry, songs, etc.

The final running order, with a great deal of help from Sue and John, was:

■ Gathering and welcome. Brief explanation of what we would be doing.

■ Walk along marked route.

■ Visit summit of hill. Windsock and red smoke.

■ Naming venue framed by bunting and banners. Accordion music and brazier for homely atmosphere.

■ The two aunts, nephew and niece gather in the flowers we had asked people to bring and form Ewan's name on the ground.

■ I explain the symbolism of the flowers.

■ A friend sings "Linden Lea"

■ My sister reads a poem.

■ Chris explains the significance of the journey and the place.

■ Our niece reads a poem from Chris's parents, who are unable to be present because of illness.

■ I lift Ewan high and we say in unison, "We name our child, Ewan Philip."

■ My father calls for a toast on behalf of the grandparents.

■ A friend sings "Dance to Your Daddy"

■ John reads a poem he has written for the occasion.

■ Children are each given a "telescope" to help find our way back to the cars and to the hall for tea.

We had lots of very positive responses to the Naming:

"I thought there was going to be a vicar and we would have to hand the flowers to him. This was much better." (One of the younger guests).

"Although we are Christians, because it wasn't a christening we thought much more about it."

"It was so much more personal than many ceremonies."

"I wish we had known about Namings when our children were young"

"If we ever have kids, we should do something like this."

We had been warned that some guests, particularly older ones, might be apprehensive about a Naming and that we should talk it through with them. My sister said that the style of the invitation (featuring the silhouette of a wind-bent hawthorn) put some of her friends in mind of occult goings-on. We also had some Christian friends asking – light-heartedly – "There's nothing pagan about it is there?" I confirmed that we were only biting chicken's heads off. But on the whole this wasn't a problem.

On the practical side, we found that having a third party helped us make our decisions more quickly and amicably!

We found it very easy to forget nitty-gritty details like not giving out sheets of paper which might blow away in the wind and making sure there was someone there to open up the hall afterwards for refreshments. It was important to delegate as many jobs as possible: photography and video-ing, cattle monitor, assistance with rigging.

It is also important to make the event your own, to draw on the talents of your friends and yourselves as far as possible. We have many happy memories of the day.

In these fingers, in these hands

In these fingers, in these hands,
let there be life,
let there be growing, reaching out,
sowing and reaping,
let there be healing,
from the strength in these hands.

In these fingers, in these hands,
across the shimmering lands,
the raging seas, and dark rain forests,
Arctic ice, and desert sands,
the whole earth,
from these strong hands
let there be triumphant life!

For ever and ever!

Nellie Dodsworth, 1904-1978

Naming Peter William Ashburner

Brian and Susan wanted to say thank-you for Peter, their first child, and wanted a formal acknowledgement that Peter has come into the world.

As people with strong moral views, they feel embarrassed using ceremonies that they do not believe in. A christening service was not appropriate for them, as they do not accept Christian links with original sin, preferring to see the new-born as innocent and pure. Baptism in the Christian church involves making very definite promises on behalf of the child, which can be seen by the parents as inappropriate.

They came to Welfare State International for advice about how to create a public ceremony which would be a celebration of the gift of the life of Peter. They also wished to incorporate a statement about their intention to do their best to ensure that Peter acquires a moral sense. Although they were not using a traditional religious ceremony they were anxious that what they replaced it with would not lack rigour, would still lend significance to the occasion, would have the right emphasis and would show respect for the child. Without wishing to impose beliefs, values or expectations on Peter, they are seeking an environment in which he will journey through life to reach his chosen goal.

They live in a fine house with its own garden, adjacent to fields, a river and the village church. They fixed on a weekend gathering of extended family and friends at the house, beginning from 2 pm Saturday afternoon and continuing over Sunday to allow relaxed time for celebration and walking, cycling, pony rides, kite flying and feasting.

The ceremony was at 5 pm Saturday in the garden. Since moving into the house they had been underway with the creation of their own stone circle in the garden. They chose to leave the task of placing the last stone until the naming day so that others could participate in this work as part of the ceremony.

They sent out an invitation and programme in advance which gave an idea of the timing and order of events, and which in its design set the tone and atmosphere. Included in this was a "cast of characters", listing very clearly certain people's names and roles which is an excellent way of acknowledging and valuing key people to the wider group of guests and friends.

Cast of Characters

Peter William Ashburner. . . . . As the new-born
William and Dorothy Ashburner;
Pat and Bob Wilson. . . . . As the grand-parents
Richard and Joyce Ashburner;
Clare and Stewart Benson . . . . As the aunts and uncles
Jake and Kirsty Benson . . . . As the cousins
Jamie Bennett and Lynne Tyson. . . . . As the spiritual mentors
Isobel, Billy, Rod and Heather . . . . As the family of the mentors
Susan and Brian Ashburner. . . . . As the parents
Texas the dog. . . . . As the bringer of chaos
Dominic on trumpet and Kate on fiddle . . . . As bringers of fanfares and
serenades to lift the heart
Glenn and Mandy. . . . . As keepers of the barbecue and
as source of all sustenance
Arthur. . . . . As provider of alcoholic beverages and toasts

Brian wrote afterwards

"The best bit was getting everyone to write a wish or a piece of wisdom for Peter on a thin sheet of copper (they were tags from a garden centre). Then all were put in a pot which was buried beneath a standing stone which we erected in a (pre-dug) hole. It got everyone involved and into the spirit of the occasion. We were very lucky with the weather, which was superb ... PS The idea is that copper will last a long time in the ground."

It is of course possible to substitute the planting of a young tree with significant objects or container buried underneath.

If the term 'spiritual mentors' doesn't feel right, consider alternative language for god-parents, such as supporting adults, spiritual parents etc.).

Naming Ceremony for 7 Children

Lois Lambert, a Welfare State associate, tells of this naming ceremony mounted in 1979. A team of seven or eight artists worked for a week on the project.

On Easter six families and their guests gathered to celebrate the naming of seven children in the grounds of Duncombe Park in North Yorkshire. As we collected ourselves under the high cupola of the Tuscan Temple, many of us still strangers to each other, we looked forward to the day with a mixture of feelings. Some of us had been involved in the preparations

Boris Howarth

during the previous week; building a giant of earth and stone in the woods, making and rehearsing a shadow play, erecting a huge bird whose wings spanned a wide avenue, whitewashing the old orangery where the feast was to be held, and killing and cooking the pig which would be served at it. Some of us knew the order of events. All of us welcomed the chance to dedicate our children in front of friends and strangers, a gesture of hope and blessing, protection too, in the face of the terrors of our present world ...

Our child, Richard, who was to be named, was a lad of eight, and we had chosen him for our son when he was four months old. So this ceremony of dedication was especially important to my husband David and myself, since we had not been present at his birth ... We wondered how Richard, old enough to play a conscious role in his naming ceremony, would handle the day.

We had driven together to Duncombe Park, and as we stood under the dome waiting for everyone to gather, there was a sense of being outside the usual boundaries of time. It had been a steep climb to reach this spot from the cars, and at the top there was an unexpected landscape that was at once natural and artificial. A wide grass walk opened out in front of us, bordered by unkempt woods on one side and tidy rows of evergreens on the other – a long vista with a Greek Temple at its end, towards which we walked slowly chatting to those we knew and also to one or two we didn't. The children played around us, excited by the space, and with us also was a great grandmother of 92, who had come to take part in the naming of her great-grandson George.

Three musicians awaited us at the Greek Temple and led us toward a tented space where we were to be shown a shadow play. With them, carried on his father's back, was six months old Hannes, also to be named that day, who jumped up and down in his papoose trying to grasp the bird's nest in his mother's hat as she played the saxophone. The family had come from Holland and already there was a sense in which we all felt that we were on a journey together, having come from very different directions. This feeling was reinforced by the shadow play in the darkened tent, where we were all brought together in a small space for the first completely directed moment. It was the story of Gilgamesh and his search for Eternal Youth; he finds it, but loses it to a serpent who finds it tasty, changes his skin and vanishes in thick grey swamps forever. So Gilgamesh lost Eternal Youth but found the salt of Life sweeter and danced with Death in Joy and Pain and Wonder.

For most of us this was our first experience of a shadow play and the moving images on the white screen lit by flaming torches had a subtle effect on us as a group; the tent seemed like a portal to another world where rare and magical things could happen. Jamie Proud explained that we were now embarking on the next stage of our journey – a Quest through the elements. Now, for the first time, we entered an area that was not tamed or landscaped. Having climbed with some difficulty up into the woods which bordered the tent, we had not gone very deep into the woods when we found ourselves approaching a tree which spread its branches to form a dome, under which creatures of all sizes and shapes grown naturally out of wood and moss had been gathered

"Noah dropped his telescope among the old certificates in the cupboard
And muddied his boots on the new found land
But the eager angels still rode the surf
And the speckled dew, like fishes' eyes
Flashed beneath the indifferent stars;
Rain washed the diamond roads
and flowers sang the pungent breeze.
When the new morning rain had come
and gone again by dinner time,
Noah smiled in his cup and replanted the everlasting vine."

together and placed in a forest of jagged perspex pieces. Above them the trees suddenly became a spring and all the branches came alive with streams of water.

Boris Howarth (who had planned the day) had written a short dedication for this space, which Jamie delivered like a familiar fireside story:

"Noah dropped his telescope ..."

Some went forward and cupped water in their hands to drink, or washed their baby's hands or face; others seemed to decide that this was after all a space to dream in. No one told us what to do as we listened to the water cascading down from the branches of the tree, and at this stage I sensed an uncertainty as to what, if anything, was required of us.

Now we followed the musicians to a huge recumbent giant built of earth and stone, with a smoking pit of a stomach. Here there was no such uncertainty; taut fishing rods, one for each child, reached into his smouldering belly and one by one the parents pulled out a paper gift; a winged ship, a lighthouse, a dove. Richard and four year old Kylie Stark were able to do their own fishing, but they needed parental help with the heavy twelve foot rods, and there was laughter and supportive cheers as each child struggled to free the gift from the giant man.

Here too there was a story for us:

From the earth man we wound our way through the trees to a cleared circle where stood a kiln about four feet high and three feet in diameter, built of twigs and bundles of straw to form a delicate criss-cross pattern. It was topped with a nest ... As we approached, the kiln was fired, and as the flames licked the nest each family was given a brightly painted egg of paper and sawdust and invited to place it in the nest.

"There is a land of men
base-metal in their groins,
Where no mortal treads. Upon
their shoulders
Perfection flutters like a silver
bird.
The shadow of hunting does
not stain their pure breath.
Sometimes this God-fired
jungle flames with newer life:
Phantom tigers tremble on the
brink of dark pools
Which reflect the lolling eye of
greater heavens."

"Come back later and see what hatches,"

we were told.

"Burning apples fall from orchards where not even God has been
And from the sawdust egg the terracotta of our hearts
Wings forth and beats the sullen air anew."

Water, earth, and fire; we went on our way with a sense of having set something in motion. We soon found ourselves in a high wide avenue across which stretched the wings of a huge white bird. Here we took our children forward and holding them high in our arms we made the declaration of names:

"Richard Soyinka Lambert
May you dance in your visions
May you sing your dancing visions to the world."

Our hearts were full as we watched each child held high and heard the names echo in that space of air:

"Hall George Daedalus Vanbrugh Howarth
Kylie Ann Stark
Hannes Antonius Van Raay
Bryony Stroud Watson
Katherine Bronia Witts
Thomas Christopher Llewellyn Witts
May their names sing as long as these brave trees
May their lives echo on in the stars
May our love give them help as they travel alone
May our prayers hold their hand as they fly."

As each name rang out a rocket exploded into the sky. Each stage of this gentle journey seemed to have been preparing us for this moment.

"In the company of those we love
Of friends who warm us
And strangers who augment our little world
We name our children."

Then followed a grand feast, a treasure hunt for the children and finally, the concluding action, the liberation of doves. We parted from each other having travelled together through territory that we do not often negotiate in our society, which packages and parcels out our experiences for us so that we lose touch with all that is profound or disturbing in our lives. We had confirmed and celebrated our shared humanity, making a public declaration of our love, our hopes for our children. There had been nothing strange or mystical about the day, we had not been seeking for a powerful magic in which to lose ourselves. All day there had been plenty of time to talk, to explain, to experience each focused moment in our own time ... Nothing had been too much trouble for this celebration and every element of it had been prepared with care for this afternoon alone – the decorations in the orangery, the shadow play, the images and spaces in the woods, even the two chemical toilets which we had of necessity to erect in the woods, had been made as magnificent as possible, with white drapes, foliage and flowers.

**Ron Grimes of the Department of Religion & Culture,
Wilfrid Laurier University, Waterloo, Ontario, Canada says:**

Although the telling of this previous rite is straightforward, the power of its imagery is considerable. The prose evokes the wonder of the event, which is no small feat, since ritual accounts are so often schematic and boring. The poetry is integral to the rite, not merely something added to it, and the poetry lies as much in the way places and objects are crafted as in the way the poems are written. It is not uncommon for poetry to be included in rites of passage, especially weddings, but it is rare that the rhythm and structure of the actions and places are as poetic as the poetry. As a result, poetry laid into Western rites of passage tends to dangle, calling attention to itself. We in the contemporary West tend to segregate poetry and ritual into separate domains, the one, literary, the other, religious. Outside the dominant religious traditions, when poetry does makes its way into ritual, the temptation is to use poetry to levitate participants into realms precious and supposedly profound. This way of trying to unite poetry and ritual all too often fails. Here, the poetry is not severed from outdoor chemical toilets, from huffing and puffing up hills, from the prose of explaining what this action or that thing means. Like buildings in which air ducts and electrical wiring are left as a visible part of the decor, this rite's bones are sticking out. Rather than violating the aesthetic, they are made an integral part of the ritualizing. There is no mystification of power and no pseudo-magical conjuration. But magic there is – the magic of the everyday made special by the concentration of human energies and affections.

By being celebrated on Easter, this naming ceremony co-opts the sacrality of the season, but it refuses to be shackled by either the Christian liturgical calendar or conventional uses of the Bible. Biblical characters appear, but burning apples fall from orchards where not even God has been. He is not omnipresent or all powerful. Noah and God are cast in uncharacteristic roles played in spaces decidedly pagan or secular. There is no sense that the children should make way for these patriarchs, that their naming fest should really be transmuted into worship instead.

The age range of the children is considerable, and the rite is not driven by a rigid sense of timing which would insist that naming must coincide with birth or necessarily occur at a specific age. So the social and ritual structures are loose, and the ideology that would rationalize the actions is downplayed. We are never told why these children are being named. Likely, they already have names, and some have been using them for quite some time. Never mind, this is an occasion upon which the children's lives become centers of sustained, collective, celebrative, adult attention. Who could ask for more? If the named children were too young to remember the events, the chances are that the adults will both recollect and retell the story, and the story will then do some of the work of spiritual formation.

Kylie Stark, who was three years old when the Duncombe Park ceremony was performed, is now an arts professional in her 20s. She recollects it this way:

I remember nothing of the poetry or the stories, and few of the images. My overall impressions are emotional – excitement, confusion, a feeling of expectation. I remember the surroundings, the lush green woods and the tree which wept, but the two most vivid images are of doves. At home I have a small clay dove which I picked out from the kiln at some point in the ceremony. It has travelled around the world with me in a backpack; it travels with me to this day. At the time, I was delighted to be given a present. As I grew older, I endowed it with mystical powers due to the unusual circumstances from whence it came. Now it is a physical confirmation that the day actually existed. The most specific memory I have from the actual ceremony is of being given a live dove to release to the winds. I distinctly remember the thrill of holding the bird, the excitement of letting it go, and watching it fly away, followed swiftly by disappointment that it had gone forever.

When people asked about the naming ceremony, I often replied, blithely and without thinking much, that I had to walk through fire and water and let go of a dove. Only when I travelled to Bali and witnessed the cultural importance of ritual in all aspects of life there, did I really begin to question and to think about what the naming ceremony actually meant to me. It was a celebration of new life and a way of welcoming children into the natural world. It brought together people who were not committed to the beliefs of a particular religion, and it enabled them to "christen" their children. Obviously, a celebration can be done in many ways, but the basic ideas of fire, air, and water, along with the dove as a representation of freedom, gives the ceremony a sense of cohesion and simplicity without the need for ritualized movements or incantations. I may have idealized the experience, forgotten the cold wind and sense of uncertainty and misdirection. Perhaps I have even invented some aspects of it, but the ideas and feelings behind the naming ceremony remain, for me, brilliant and beautiful.

Ceremony at Nimbin, Australia

Jenny Dell wrote this description for the Nimbin News in New South Wales in January 1979.

Christenings and naming ceremonies can often be self-conscious and precious affairs, but this was different, and will perhaps set a precedent for similar events to take place in Nimbin. In organising the event the Foxes used much restraint so as to leave room for the families to define their own space and use it in their own personal ways; thus the basic structure was there which ensured that it would be a delightful happening and within that structure it was what the people wanted it to be.

John Lynes opened the proceedings with an address, in which he said:

"People of Nimbin, I expect you all wonder why I've been asked to make this speech this afternoon. I can only hope that it's not only because of my grey hair, but more particularly that the old settlers see me as a semi-hippie, and the new settlers see me as a triangle, or half a square!

If that's the case, then perhaps on this New Year's Day, with the naming of these children, when we are looking at things afresh, it may be appropriate for me to talk to you. You all know of the doom that is said to have been laid on the white settlers and their progeny of Nimbin. That doom will remain on them until they become either trusting and innocent as little children or they take on the spirit of the dead Aborigines. I suspect that the latter is probably the more true interpretation of the doom.

(The Aborigines) ... adapted to the surroundings in which they lived probably as few other peoples of the Earth have adapted; but unfortunately we can't any longer just adapt to what nature provides for us. We have, for better or for worse, already made such an adaptation to the original Earth that we now have to learn to live, and adapt to what presently exists.

One other thing that was noticeable with those Aborigines was that they had strong tribal rules. Those rules were designed for the good, not of an individual but of the tribe as a whole. And I think the time has come where we in Nimbin are going to have to learn that we must work for the good of the tribe of Nimbin as a whole, not for any one part of it.

"It's like weaving a piece of cloth: when you weave

a piece of cloth the first thing you do is to set up the warp. That warp is tight, twisted hard, and it is there forming a framework. I think that the Old Settlers have provided, in our area, that warp. And we New Settlers have to provide the woof and the weft which is adaptable. It moves in and out of the warp, but when the cloth is made you'll find that both parts of it have changed, that there has been adaptation on both sides. And you end up with a piece of beautiful material. That, I think, we can do, here in Nimbin.

You may say, if we have to go back to the spirit of those dead Aborigines, that we're looking backwards, and not forwards. I don't think that's the case; I think if you see what Kahlil Gibran says on death, it will give you a picture of

Nimbin – Australia
New Year 1979

in which ...
At this changing of the years
in which
at this crossroads of awakening
The Fiddler of Fate
Meets a street band (icoot)
and farts a G seventh
That's really a beaut

in which ...
The fat grey giant
Trips on the Fire of Doom
And the cow jumps
Over the Moon (just)

in which ...
The Butler spoon stirs
In the river of Stones
And a baby sings
High in the stars

in which ...
A cream bun revolves
on a Swallow's white cloud
And a farmer danced
Off with his spouse (just)

On the last day of the Old Year of 1978, burn bad memories and old filing cabinets on the great log fire of the old Grey Giant.
(Blue Knob Hall)

Sing the praises of the floating cradle of nursery rhymes.

On the first day of the New Year of 1979, celebrate fresh beginnings with the naming of new children, the re-opening of the Bush Factory (remembering its Buttery past and celebrating its first theatre piece).

Celebrate with a wondrous tea and an afternoon parade of Fresh Carnival Cakes.

John Fox

what we are really looking for. He says: 'If you would indeed behold the spirit of death, open your heart unto the body of Life, for Life and Death are One, even as the river and the sea are One'".

John's speech was followed beautifully by Beth Freeman singing Wild Mountain Thyme ("Will ye go, lassie, go?) – a song that John Fox had wanted to include in the naming ceremony because for many of us there it evoked the memory of little Celia Singer who died last year at the age of two.

With everyone seated in a circle, shaded from the hot sun by parasols and canopies, the naming of children began. Parents were able to choose to receive a Buddhist name and blessing from Phra Khantipalo, or an Aboriginal one from Uncle Lyle Roberts, after they had taken their child into the circle and declared its given name aloud. Locks of the hair of each child had been collected; half of each lock was buried under a tree that was planted for the occasion, and the other half tied to helium balloons, which at the end of the naming were ceremoniously released by Uncle Lyle, Khantipalo and John Lynes.

Fourteen pigeons had been caged, one for each child, and after the naming they were released one by one; the children were delighted as "their" bird wriggled in their hand, and on release, soared away with a fluttering of wings, to freedom.

Uncle Lyle Roberts and Albury Roberts (the second elder, after Uncle Lyle, of the Bunjalung Tribe) sang a ceremonial song and performed a dance which many may not have understood but we were highly privileged to watch, and may never see again. By their presence there, the Aboriginal elders may be said to be validating our presence ... validating our presence in Nimbin and perhaps giving us some support in averting the doom of which John Lynes spoke.

The children were named with many blessings from different cultures; perhaps a little of each blessing is encapsulated in the delightful words that Jani and Mike Shegog wrote for their infant daughter Amber, and spoke for her in the circle:

"If we could gather pieces of virgin nature
evergreen timeless untouched as before the time
of whiteman coming to this land

we would conceal every timepiece
sundial or shadow and holding your hand
we would take you there
and set you free

... to grow".

What I feel about having had a Naming Ceremony

I've sort of been in the middle of two. The first was entirely mine, and it was then, as a baby, that I received my name. The second, maybe five or six years later, was a ceremonial day to name several other children, but I was able to take part in the activities. I mention both because they each meant and mean such different things to me.

The first ceremony was in 1971. Secular namings were unusual things at this time. There was little to compare anything to, to share ideas with or to borrow a structure from. The "organisers" (the babies' parents and their friends) performed a brave thing. It was radical and on the edge. They went for it, took it seriously, and meant what they did, but also knew it was sufficiently weird to make a powerful, political impression on those gathered. I understand that a real live goat, a mock priest, a greasepaint jester and a baby were involved. I was the baby. It was a performance with a public audience, not a private ceremony with gathered friends. On this occasion it was the friends as a clan creating an artwork on life as a statement to those on the outside. It served a function – to give me a name, and was a rite of passage for those creators who felt the need to perform these life markers with incredible originality and personal meaning. They were learning and pushing and receiving something new and fresh, just as I was. But I think in many ways it had little to do with that baby, with me, my being or the life that lay ahead. We say this now of regular christenings ... how odd! My naming was alternative but how personal was it? Was it an experiment and a statement or a genuine gift to the child?

The second naming ceremony I remember more clearly, and I think it served several child-centred functions very well. The children involved were older, they were participants not just helpless targets of goodwill (or in my case anarchy!) and were able to partially make decisions. Each child shared a secret name with their parents, sent a tiny lantern boat bobbing away down a cavernous underground stream and released a pigeon into the sky. Although feeling a bit left out of the "receiving a name" part, I was thrilled to be able to release a pigeon from my own hands. This sort of involvement from the child gives them a role, makes them feel important and a necessary member of the gathering. It is wonderful to give a child a day focussed entirely on them and their lives, with hopes for the future and the undeniable bond created with all those gathered around them.

Hannah Fox

The Role of Naming in Stillbirths

Immediately after a miscarriage or stillbirth, hospital staff strive to offer care and support to bereaved parents, to preserve the dignity and poignancy of the experience and to initiate the difficult process of mourning.

When a baby dies during labour/delivery or immediately afterwards, parents should be told at once.

A baby should be certified as having been born alive if there are any signs of life at all, even near the limits of viability. The parents will then have a proper birth certificate and death certificate for their baby.

Naming the baby

Parents may want to name their baby (if they have not already done so). Once they have decided on a name, some may want the hospital chaplain, or another religious adviser, to give a blessing or say prayers for their baby by name.

Staff should ask parents whether they may use the baby's name. If there is no name, then it is important to speak of your baby (or "little one" or any other affectionate term). "The" baby is very impersonal.

Naming can be important, even for parents who have had an early miscarriage. It helps to give a focus to ideas about the baby. It is easier to choose a name if the baby's sex is known and this should always be recorded if it is possible to tell. But parents may still want to give their baby a name even if it is impossible to know the baby's sex.

Funeral

Many parents will want to make arrangements for a funeral or some other kind of ceremony for their baby. Others will be pleased if this possibility is suggested to them. They will need information to help them plan what is right for them.

Creating memories

Parents may want to gather mementoes such as their baby's cot card, name band, locks of hair, foot or hand prints, stills from scans, a foetal monitor tracing, their baptism card, and so on. They will value anything which will help them to remember their baby.

Parents should be asked before a lock of hair is cut or a foot or handprint taken.

Involvement of other members of the family

Parents may want other members of the family, including other children, to see the baby. It is almost always helpful for siblings to see their dead brother or sister. What is imagined is often frightening: the reality can be reassuring. It can also help later if the family has shared memories to talk about.

Parents may wish to take photographs of their baby with others in their family. Photographs taken of siblings with their dead brother or sister can be helpful later, especially if they are very young at the time the baby dies.

Repeated offers/suggestions

Although parents should never feel pressured, it may be appropriate if certain offers and suggestions are gently repeated. For example, if they have not already done so, parents might be encouraged to see and/or hold their baby to give a name, to take photos or gather other mementoes. If they have at first rejected the idea of a funeral or other ceremony, they may want help to reconsider this and be sure of their decision.

"The pictures of our baby form the mainstay of our memories. Along with the cards and letters, the wristband, the footprints the midwife made us, the post mortem report, even the receipt for the funeral ... These, more than the ashes from the cremation, are the remains of our baby."

(Naomi, whose baby was stillborn)

From Guidelines for Professionals, by SANDS Stillborn and Neonatal Death Society, 1991

Ceremonies for the Reluctant

Dear Jonathan

You asked me to write you a letter about how I feel about naming ceremonies. This is a slightly confused train of thought which hopefully leads to a clear idea.

As a performer I'm very happy to be in front of hundreds of people and have always enjoyed the sense of being the centre of attention in a show but when it comes to personal celebrations I have a very different set of feelings. I deflect focus wherever possible and have consistently avoided big events for birthdays and other personal marking points in my life. I have often felt guilty as close friends and relations have wanted to make more of my birthdays but in the end they have been days for me so I have chosen minimal fuss. I don't know where this comes from and have given up trying to change my personality to fit with other people's expectations.

I think that this also was one of the reasons why none of my children have really had an official "naming". However it is something I have often thought and talked about. The closest I came was in a very informal way walking on the beach with Rosie and Mary on Portobello Beach in Edinburgh.

We drew Rosie's name in the sand and I remember feeling that it was a good moment, a sense of a naming ... only slightly acknowledged ... and I have a photo ... Then when I was on holiday with Marion, Joe and Manuela in Ireland we were walking on a beach in County Cork and we all wrote our names (maybe I didn't do mine ...!) and that felt like a similar moment ... I like the idea of the names being washed and worn away by the weather ...

I do believe passionately in alternative celebrations and finding a way of creating home-made celebrations. Many of my favourite and most powerful occasions as a musician have

been at friends' funerals, birthdays and weddings.
And now I think that my children have missed out on
something and wonder whether there is something new I can
do now. They all have different parentage but I have always
made little of that ... Now they would all
need separate ceremonies according to their age ...

A naming should give a child a sense of their place in the
complex web of relationships that can support, challenge,
strengthen them over many years. It is about affirming a
network of unconditional love ... It is a celebration by all of the
people involved and it can be small and simple or much more
complex ...

A journey to visit people would be ideal ... ten days and ten
people ... It would be a way of giving a focus that wouldn't
embarrass a child moving into self-conscious teenage years.
Not a trip down memory lane but it should register the past
and show a line of connections to make for the future ...
I can't decide now how to choose the people but I guess they
are a mixture of family and friends. It could be like a magical
mystery tour where you don't necessarily meet the people in
expected places. It could also be planned together so there
were few surprises. A mixture of the two would make it feel
both secure and also an adventure. Associated with the
journey I can imagine a documentation with photos, gifts,
drawings and pieces of music.

I hope that it will give my children a clear set of lines of
support that they feel they can use as they go through the
next period of their lives. And for me it would give a series of
powerful meetings in an intimate and supportive atmosphere.
That's the plan ... I'll keep you in touch as the journeys develop
and become a reality.

Yours, Pete Moser

Story of a Renaming – Sue Gill

In my mid-forties it occurred to me that I had never had a name that I felt any strong attachment to. I was Miss Susan Robinson, then Mrs Susan Fox. The two surnames were fine in themselves, and great for other people, but somehow nothing to do with me – coming as they did, from my father and my husband.

At the moment these thoughts crystallised in my mind, I realised that I could have a name of my own, and I knew straightaway what it should be.

I had found my spot, my home and that place is The Gill. I would be Sue Gill – that felt right and positive. I could own this name. I have lived here with my family for several years already, and can find no reason to think of leaving.

I did not negotiate it well with John, my husband, and he was, understandably, quite threatened by it. For nearly twenty years we had worked together in the arts company we founded.

There's a prejudice around "the wife" being associated with a business or an enterprise or an organisation. Culturally, people of my generation assume the man would be leading it and "the wife" is there on sufferance. It's a woman's thing, lacking in assertiveness, a quiet gnawing apology, however useful a contribution that person is making.

Changing my name and nothing else, dissolved all that overnight. New people met me in my own right, and maybe later learnt I am married to John. Inevitably, people who already knew us thought we must have split up. That had to be dealt with, patiently over the years.

I have never regretted it – although I failed as far as my own parents' true understanding of the change. Fearing to hurt them through any kind of rejection and hating confrontation, I left them believing that because I work in the arts, it must be some sort of a stage name. Moral cowardice on my part.

My track record with rites of passage demanded that I, as a middle-aged woman, had a naming ceremony. I bottled out at the thought of summoning all my friends, colleagues and family, not wishing to be the centre of attention. I left it, and just dithered for a while, but knew that one day ...

Then the perfect impromptu occasion offered itself. We were having a party on The Gill, in the old Sunday School, to say farewell to a popular young couple who were leaving with a certain reluctance on account of job promotion. Neighbours had come together, made the food, decorated the hall and some were playing music together. I realised there would never be a better opportunity than this one, with my own family and my immediate community as witnesses. Without wishing to eclipse the party, I said I wanted to make an announcement.

Unprepared, and without a script, I just stood up. (I would not recommend this!). I announced that I felt I wanted to change my name and why, and how I saw the significance of it for myself. I said that this was the perfect occasion to break the news and they were the first to hear, ending with "and from today I should like to be known as Sue Gill." People were pleased for me, and quite moved by the choice, and very supportive.

A week later I was at my laconic solicitor's desk, signing to make it all legal by Deed Poll. It felt an important rite of passage. All he could say was "It doesn't make any difference to me. You can call yourself Mickey Mouse if you want!"

A CELTIC BENEDICTION
OR WELL-WISHING

The peace of the running water to you,

The peace of the flowing air to you,

The peace of the quiet earth to you,

The peace of the shining stars to you,

And the love and the care of us all to you.

PART FIVE
NUTS AND BOLTS

Logistics: When, Where, Who, and What?

Resources

People to help

Be bold and ask for help. Make it clear that if people are thinking about giving you, or the baby, a gift, what you would really appreciate is the gift of their time in the preparation of the ceremony.

Maybe a couple of hours on the computer to type up and lay out beautifully your scribbled notes of what you plan to say on the day, or an order of the ceremony with copies of poems and readings, for people to take away.

There may be some administration – sending out maps and travel directions, sending out lists of local B&Bs, that friends could help with.

On the day, to have a right-hand person whose job it is to keep everything ticking over, and who would get pleasure from that, would save you headaches. This is the person who identifies car parking, who picks up the key to the community centre or hall and opens up for the caterers or who remembers to switch the urn on so everything is ready when the guests arrive, and who, very possibly, gets volunteers to help clear up afterwards, deals with rubbish, makes any payments on your behalf, *and takes the keys back!*

The venue you choose, indoor or outdoor, needs access to toilets, parking, some seating maybe for older relatives (even if it is a couple of folding chairs). If you are in the landscape, say a coastal headland with a panoramic view, or under a tree or on a bridge – will there be other people/strangers around, and how do you feel about this? If you are using your back garden, think about mentioning it to your neighbours so they understand what is happening. Could they avoid cutting their grass or revving up the motorbike during the ceremony?

Elements: Air, Water, Fire and Earth

Birds You may feel the release of a dove, or pigeon, would make a fitting end to your ceremony. Libraries have contacts for local pigeon breeders, who are usually happy to bring along a basket with two or three birds in. The birds must be released in daylight – then they will fly home, out of sight, to their pigeon loft. Once it gets near dusk, they will simply circle around and roost in the nearest tree, which spoils the symbolism.

Boats You may wish to mark the start of your child's journey through life with the launch of a small handmade boat – or of several named boats, if a few children are to be named on the same day. This is fun and is exciting and a great way to send off wishes, but is a *risk*. The possibility of foundering and getting into difficulties may be seen, by some, as a bad omen. Plan this carefully. Choose your stretch of stream or river. Have an adult in wellies with a pole, or something, to avert disaster.

Kites These can make a wonderful gift and, according to the imagery, play a strong part in the imagery of a ceremony in the open air.

Fire A bonfire to gather around is always good, however small, and you could throw on aromatic herbs, once it has died down – juniper clippings, bunches of sage, rosemary, fresh cut bay leaves. The mythology of plants may well suggest something appropriate.

Flowers Ask each guest to bring along just one flower – ideally local and in season. Use them to mark out a special area for the ceremony (other children love to do this) or to spell out the child's name on the grass. The choice of a particular flower as their naming flower, honeysuckle for example, can take on significance during the rest of the child's life. Make sure you keep one or two blossoms and press them or preserve them in some way.

A toast Malt whisky, jasmine tea or organic oak leaf wine? Everyone is different, and there will be something that springs to mind that is right for you. When to do it? So you do not risk disturbing the flow of the ceremony, wait until after the announcement of the child's name and any poems, songs or tributes, before you hand round a drink. The celebrant can indicate your intention to do this – maybe proud grandparent may pop the cork. It could take a few minutes, but that's fine. People will be more relaxed once the ceremony is drawing to an end, and toasting the child is a good way to include everyone and draw things to a close. If you plan to create a "certificate" as part of the ceremony (perhaps recording the words that are spoken) then you could hand out drinks while this is being signed.

Time of Year

All things being equal (no frail relatives, no-one about to emigrate to Australia ...) it does not matter what time of year you choose. Take as long as you wish and you need to prepare, unless you have cultural traditions which indicate otherwise. Usually, there's no rush.

Allow yourself, as a new parent, to get over the initial sleepless nights and find your feet, so you have energy and space in your day to prepare the ceremony. It is important to look forward to it and to spending time with the gathering of family and friends.

The case for a spring/summer ceremony

- Can have an "active" outdoor event.

- Friends who are attending can camp or bring a caravan, to save costs.

- Good for a family picnic, walk or barbeque afterwards.

- Easier to include elements of earth, air, fire and water.

- Good for flowers, flags, kites, small boats.

- You will feel more relaxed taking your new baby out in good weather.

- Other children can run around and let off steam, with games, such as treasure hunts, as part of the day.

- Strawberry teas and home-made lemonade or elderflower champagne.

The case for an autumn/winter ceremony

- For those who would prefer to gather in a hall or a hotel for a tea party.

- The weather on the day will not affect the ceremony.

- You could bring your extended family together by renting a self-catering holiday house or cottage (out of high season) so the adults spend time together as well.

- It may be getting dark while you are celebrating the naming, so that suggests toffee apples, fireworks, lanterns, mulled wine and storytelling.

- Best season for tree planting.

- Decoration using autumn berries, candles.

- Snow!

Role of the Celebrant

You have three choices: do it yourself; invite a suitable friend, colleague or relative; use a "professional". Finding and choosing a celebrant is dealt with in Part Four: Logistics.

Usually, the celebrant is involved in advising during the drawing up of the ceremony, as well as the delivery of it on the day.

The celebrant can be seen as the master/mistress of ceremonies, who will lead the ceremony, give other contributors their cues and take the congregation/guests through, stage by stage. It is important to remember that most people have been to several weddings, funerals and possibly christenings. They know the script, where and when to sit and stand, what to expect, how long it lasts and when it has come to an end. When we invite them to a baby naming where there is no sign of the minister, no organ, no font, they can feel lost and ill at ease, therefore maybe embarrassed and almost certainly on the defensive. Secretly they may feel that your ceremony is really just a weird party, particularly if it is in the open air.

The celebrant can gather people from an informal mingling, invite them to the actual place where the heart of the ceremony will take place. He/she can frame the event, with some words on the significance of this rite of passage, indicate what is about to happen and roughly how long it will take. Frequently they will speak about the choices you have made – why is it in this particular place, what meaning does the ceremony have for the parent(s) and why do they place a value on the presence of these guests.

It is likely that the celebrant will not "name" the child themselves, but create the atmosphere and the moment into which the parent(s) can step to make the declaration and announce the names of the child.

The celebrant can cue the handing round of drinks for a toast, the exchange of gifts, and can remind people there may be a special book to write contributions in.

Afterwards, they can be a focus for comment and reaction, and they can even precipitate this in an informal conversation over refreshments. It is frequently observed that relatives who may have had doubts beforehand express comments that are entirely positive afterwards. People who never believed it possible experience something that they acknowledge was moving, meaningful, unique and unforgettable.

The ceremony may have been very short in itself – ten to fifteen minutes even – and simple in its form, but witnessing the sincerity and depth of personal expression is a moving experience.

The varied life of a British Humanist Association Officiant

Parents love their children. This urge to do the best possible for our children exists in all communities and is expressed in different cultural forms. In the world today we are constantly aware of examples of different traditions and their rituals surrounding birth, naming, entry into adolesence, marriage and death. But these traditions are not fixed. All cultural traditions have been created by people, people making choices about the forms they decide to adopt in their expression of deeply held feelings. In my work as an officiant of the BHA I contribute to the creation of ceremonies, thereby creating new traditions for the people who want them. I create ceremonies which contain what people want. Particular relatives may be mentioned or non-biological families created as the ceremony creates new social families.

So, at Nick and Sonia's wedding this June, it is Sonia's two teenage sons and Nick's brothers who will light the candles symbolising the families they come from as they embark on their new partnership with a fourteen-month old daughter.

Single parent, Jo, alienated from her family of origin, will have her three-month old son named in a ceremony that creates a new social

---

Choosing a Celebrant

The first contact is usually by telephone, you would indicate your broad ideas for the ceremony ... Size of gathering? Informal or more elaborate? At home or in a hired venue?

Then ideally you would meet, to go over family details and particular circumstances. You would consider the text of the ceremony ensuring that all the wording is appropriate and that the whole rite feels personal and distinctive. Failing a meeting this can be done in writing or via a detailed telephone conversation.

Since welcoming a new child is, usually, a joyful event, many parents choose to speak the words themselves,

---

family to support him in his future life and her in her parenting.

With Derek and Elaine we have created a Family Celebration when they will exchange promises about how they plan to continue building their family and their four year old son and daughter of eight months will have their names confirmed and their Friend Parents named as those adults who will play a special part in supporting their growing up.

In July I will officiate at a neighbour's wedding where the bride's father will give the bride away to the groom; the couple already have a two-year old.

And I look forward to the first adoptive naming ceremony I am asked to do for lesbian, gay or heterosexual parents.

How do I manage to comfortably include such variety in these ceremonies? Because I delight in the variety of cultural forms which surround me. I relish the creativity people exercise in choosing the forms in which they want to express their commitment to their partnerships and their parenting. I want to contribute to a society which welcomes and celebrates such diversity. (Names have been changed for this article)

Lucy MacKeith – an officiant with the BHA

---

and invite contributions from other members of the family and the godparents. Most naming ceremonies take place at home – or in the grandparents' home if it offers more space. They are essentially friendly occasions yet still meaningful and special. When well prepared they have the potential of bringing a family close together.

The British Humanist Association has a network of officiants available to help plan and conduct a naming ceremony which is free from the constraints of religious belief. The Baby Naming Society also offers to find someone both to write one and to lead it, either religious or not. Welfare State International offers ½ day or full day consultancies (at Lanternhouse in Cumbria) to parents who wish to create their own naming ceremonies. They also run occasional rites of passage workshops which include naming ceremonies as one of their components. They have trained celebrants available to devise and lead ceremonies locally. Some hand-crafted artefacts are also available at Lanternhouse.

The purpose of this book is to give you the confidence to create your own naming ceremony and we know many families who have done this successfully.

What spaces to use or hire

Indoors
Most people hold the naming ceremony at home. If this is a tiny house or flat they may go to a relative's larger house, possibly one that also offers a garden or outside space.

It is possible to hire a community centre or village hall, but make sure these are not too big. You could have quite a lot of work to do on rearranging and decorating the interior so you do not feel lost and unfocussed. Later, you can push back the tables for a knees-up or a ceilidh to dance the night away.

Another option is to pick a hotel that could offer you exclusive use of a lounge or library and serve you afternoon tea. Ideally somewhere with a terrace, and with grounds or views, gives you more scope. This latter suggestion is not necessarily more expensive when you add in time and expense to gather material and transform a hall, which can be labour intensive.

Outdoors

When we invite new parents to think of a place that holds a meaning for them, they often go back to where they met or visited on romantic occasions, or where special commitments were made. The trouble with the falling-in-love factor is that this can involve long car journeys to wild and beautiful places – Cornwall, Scottish glens, the Lake District ... Logistically this becomes more challenging with a young child and a posse of relatives. Better to consider local achievable destinations such as a favourite local walk, a beauty spot, a hill, a park or a woodland then back to the house for refreshments and warmth or to a pub or restaurant. This option has the bonus of introducing the child to their home patch, to the place you have chosen to live in and bring them up in for the time being. Reassuring domestic views in the foreground from the hill above your town, plus more uplifting vistas of the ocean, the moors, the estuary, the hills or mountains behind or a vast expanse of sky can be a perfect combination. If this sort of thing matters to you, chances are you will very likely know your spot already.

Mystical sites such as stone circles are always sited in astonishing locations, and some people are drawn to them for their ceremony. Many are to be found in open countryside where there is little access problem. If English Heritage manages your chosen site, then this may be a different matter.

Processions are traditional in our spiritual life. Observances around Easter and funerals in former times required people to cover distances on foot. Pilgrimages are so powerful because, when people have something really important to undertake, they walk. This puts us back in touch with what really matters and imbues the arrival, the end result, with great significance, because we have become more centred in the process.

You can design a naming ceremony where you invite people to arrive at a designated meeting point (maps, parking and toilets are a good idea), then you gather to walk (maybe ½ mile – maximum 1 mile) to the spot you have prepared for the naming. Remind guests to wrap up warm and to wear strong shoes, and get someone to carry a couple of folding chairs and rugs if you have older relatives. Is there a decent path, or a route for a four-wheel drive for those with mobility problems? When people know what is required of them in terms of physical stamina, they can enjoy it and not fear a forced seven mile route march – even if they are townies and never go walking!

Think about the other children. Build in enticements on the way to avoid the chorus of "how much further is it?" – a glimpse of a coloured marker at the destination; signs and symbols in pebbles and twigs along the way.

Ceremonial Spaces

Creating your own ceremonial space can give a powerful, natural focus for your ceremony. The physical work of preparing, making the space can be a wonderful balance to all the *thinking* you may have been doing! In a way, while you are creating the space physically, you are allowing a space to happen inside yourself, a chance for instinct to speak, for ideas to pop out of 'nowhere'.

Creating something for oneself, starting from scratch, can take a lot of energy. "Think with your hands or fingers", ie start doing it and the answers will come.

Space is a valuable commodity, it folds down to nothing, it can contain anything. A delineated place of ceremony, well prepared and decorated, perhaps not entered until the ceremony is going to begin, has a presence and inspiration of its own that in turn informs how we are feeling; it can help all those attending to naturally quieten down and become 'present'.

All that is required at a ceremony is our individual presence for the sharing of a special place and time. This quiet 'space' is at the heart of all ceremony, it's the point at which everything and everyone comes together in a magic way. Even if a ceremony is preceded by a noisy procession with drums and brass instruments, and followed by tequila, fireworks and mayhem, there is a magic moment.

It's the moment that the betrothed kiss, the moment a child is named, the moment the toast has been proposed and glasses travel towards lips; the moment the ribbon is cut, or the champagne bursts into the bows of a ship. It's when the tears well and we lose ourselves in that powerful mixture of joy and sadness.

The trick is to extend, cultivate this moment, and that is the real ceremonial space; a combination of the physical, emotional and spiritual. All the preparations and surroundings are a vessel built to launch it in. It's a magic dreamtime outside the busy-ness of everyday life in which affirmations can be made, changes and growth acknowledged, gateways passed through and wounds healed.

Even if all you do is spring-clean a room in your house, re-arrange or remove the furniture and unnecessary clutter, open the windows for a few hours to clear the air, you have created a new space and invested it with your intention and a new energy.

Define the space with home-made decorations, hang papercuts, mobiles, make simple banners, flags and bunting. If it's after dark, you can do special things with lanterns, fairy lights and candles.

The Placenta

If you want to keep the placenta then ask your midwife to wash it in cold water, wrap it in a clean plastic bag and refrigerate it. If you're preserving it for use in a ceremony some weeks or months later then you'll need to place it in a deep freeze. Many people like to plant a tree over the placenta and this is something that will form a good focus for a ceremony. The placenta contains many useful nutrients and in many cultures it is eaten. We suspect, however, that it is of greater nutritional value to the mother than anybody else so we make no recommendations for its use as a party snack after the naming ceremony!

It's a great opportunity to involve children, especially for the naming of a new brother or sister. In fact there's something about the 'let's pretend' energy of children that can teach us an aspect of the whole process, take any unnecessary seriousness out of it. To draw a circle on the ground and call it the ceremonial space in the way that kids might push furniture together and call it a house seems to have a true ring to it! In fact, the simplest ceremonial space is instant, stand in a circle, you have made the space.

Bring nature inside: flowers, branches; weave twigs and greenery into garlands. Decorate a table as a focal point: use photographs, treasured family objects, mementoes, reminders; what binds you together?

Similarly, your garden can become a ceremonial space; flags, banners, lanterns can decorate a whole area, and if you want a dedicated space you can make a temporary 'pergola' using uprights of bamboo or cut hazel rods. Stick them in the ground, join them with festoons of papercuts, wind them down their lengths with ribbons or coloured paper. Create a special archway or entrance. Everything that might be used in the ceremony can be decorated in some way. A tree-dressing has great scope, and could be the centrepiece for the space.

It's not expensive to hire a small marquee which can serve different purposes. You can create your ceremonial space within it, a whole environment or installation! It will provide shelter, and with the sides removed, still give a sense of being outdoors.

If you have chosen a natural location, you may feel that nothing needs to be added to prepare it as a ceremonial space, but the simplest of things can be done; a circle of stones on a beach, for instance, or just take some poles and flags with you. Once, as part of a sculpture workshop for adults, a colleague of ours asked the participants to build a circular enclosure in a field using fallen branches, tall plants and stalks, dried grasses, and found objects from a nearby wood. When they'd finished, they entered through the archway that was part of the structure and sat down in the circle. The group, who had been chattering merrily all day, quickly fell silent. "It's like walking into a church," said one. "It's got a real feeling of magic to it", said another.

There is of course a very different dynamic to holding a ceremony outdoors and you may prefer to be closer to the Earth, under the sky, amongst nature. This all includes our somewhat unpredictable climate which we have to be ever philosophical about! If all the foregoing is a bit too hippiesque for you, weld together some old cars in a scrapyard, use fluorescent plastic and striplights, whatever, do it your way, in your style. This is very much about empowering ourselves, re-discovering a way of doing things together, having left it to the 'experts' for so long.

Practical Organisation and Stage Management

Creating a ceremony can have very similar requirements and logistics to putting on any event. There's a huge difference between inviting a couple of close friends round to your house for a simple ceremony and organising a ceremony that will take place out of doors, away from mains services and shelter, with fifty guests including your grandparents!

If you are taking on the whole task of devising and organising your own ceremony, be aware of how much work you may be letting yourself in for! Once you've an idea of what form your ceremony is going to take, try and visualize it all the way through from the moment your guests arrive to when the last ones leave; and then there's the washing up! Think through the nuts and bolts, work out how long it will take to organise and allow plenty of time for unforeseen things.

To enjoy and fully partake in the ceremony, people need to be undistracted, physically comfortable, and generally at ease. Children need to be accommodated, people need to eat, drink, go to the toilet, be sheltered from the weather, and so on.

In general, especially for a ceremony you have created for yourself, someone needs to lead it; be it yourself or somebody chosen by you. The celebrant or Master of Ceremonies (MC) is there not only to conduct the ceremony, but to guide everyone through: one real source of unease is not knowing what to do or where to go.

The MC can explain the proceedings clearly; you may have a script or running order. There's nothing wrong with the MC explaining the ceremony as it happens. It might also be helpful to explain to those present that nobody is going to be expected to do anything that makes them feel uncomfortable. Remember that a home-made ceremony is still very much breaking new ground; if your guests are a real cross-section of people, there may be some wild preconceptions floating around! Put people at ease.

If you wish to arrange everybody formally for the actual ceremony, which may only last a few minutes, a circle is a universal way of investing everybody present with equal involvement and responsibility; nobody is standing at the back, nobody is standing at the front. On the other hand your ceremony may not call for this; naming a house for instance, might involve a walking round, a perambulation.

How to Dress the Child

My neighbours, Carol and George, invited several of us in for a drink one evening, on the occasion of their Silver Wedding anniversary. Inevitably, the photographs came out – George with long hair and lapels – to much laughter. The next thing I knew, Carol was handing around a small ornate garment, trimmed with white fur around the hem. It was then that the story came out.

Carol's mother, before she was married, bought a length of cream brocade with a gold thread design on it, intending it to be made into her own wedding dress. She was forbidden to pursue this dream, and was married in a white dress. Twenty years later, Carol, the daughter, used the cloth for her own wedding dress, then a couple of years later, in a cut-down version, it became the christening robe for her daughter, then for her son. She has kept it, although there seems no signs, from her grown up children, of her becoming a grandmother for some time.

This mirrors the traditions around the three-tier wedding cake. One to cut and serve on the wedding day, one to cut up and send to those unable to attend the wedding, and the third to keep (for a year or so?) for the christening cake.

In terms of garments for a naming ceremony, there may be some special fabric that has a significance within a family that is appropriate to use to dress the child. In these days of dungarees, bib and brace, leggings and shirts and mini-skirts, often in fluorescent colours, the "robe" needs some justifying. A special waistcoat or jerkin over the usual stretchy baby all-in-ones, or a handmade hat, can feel quite ceremonial. Ethnic craft shops have irresistible little garments from all parts of the world.

With the technology in the High Street to print our own T-shirts, there's a possibility of customising a length of cloth for a "shawl" or wrap for a baby or designing a special sweatshirt or little jacket for a young child. Give it some thought – and if the child is of any age, consult them too. The "Bride of Christ" white outfits that we see so readily for first communion do not usually have a role in a secular naming ceremony. Colours may reflect the seasons. Style of outfit should reflect the location, first and foremost. If you are on the shores of a lake, probably a fleecy duffle coat is the perfect choice ... and nowadays they come in fun colours.

If the ceremony is to be held outdoors, adequate provision for weather has to be made, even if it's just reminding people to bring a thermos flask and a cagoule. If you're going to delineate a ceremonial space, don't forget to work out how much room you need for everyone to stand or sit comfortably.

And finally, after you've carefully prepared everything, there comes a point where whatever happens, happens. We're living in an unpredictable universe; if something goes wrong, it's not a 'bad omen' ! If there's rain going down the back of your neck after the forecast was sunshine, just look upon it as the cleansing, purifying element of water blessing your ceremony! Do the ceremony, then dive for cover, giggling!

Documentation

Documentation of an event can take many forms and will only be limited by your imagination. The question to ask is why are you wanting to document the event in the first place? It may be that you are trying to convey something of the atmosphere to friends and/or relatives who could not make it on the day. Perhaps you want a way for you and your family to be able to relive the event later.

The naming ceremony of a young child also brings all sorts of possibilities for creating a documentary memento which can be presented to them at a later rite of passage – perhaps their 18th birthday. There is something very extraordinary about suddenly coming upon evidence of some half-remembered event from one's childhood, but the trick to this is that the item must be created at the time and then strictly hidden away for the intervening decades. If you watch a video of your christening again and again from your early childhood onwards then not just the tape will get "worn out".

The most important part of any "recording" activity is finding a balance between advance planning and being able to react to opportunities that come up on the day. In all the formats described below you'll need to think ahead about what you're trying to achieve but at the same time be alert to other possibilities that come up spontaneously.

Photographs

Get somebody else to take the official ones, it might be a professional photographer or a keen friend. Be sure to confirm with them

- what style of photographs that you want (formal/candid etc) and whether there are definite aspects of the ceremony to be included (will a camera flash be intrusive?)

- if there are certain "set-piece" shots that you definitely want (eg whole group; grandparents holding the baby).

You'll probably want to put together your own album with the resulting photos. Friends may also send you photographs that they have taken themselves. Why not positively encourage this and invite people to contribute. In this way the document becomes less of a formal photo-album and more of a scrapbook

Wall art

You don't have to produce something that ends up in a bound form, why not make something that will go on a wall? This is an ideal way to incorporate older brothers and sisters, although it may be best to invite them to contribute to a poster rather than to manage the whole process themselves! If you want something that will last a bit longer then go for the ubiquitous (but very effective) framed photo-collage. Remember to create a focus for the collage – perhaps an enlarged photo of the baby – otherwise the viewer's eye will not be drawn into the picture.

If you have the computer equipment and you're feeling very ambitious then you might even produce a photo-montage in a programme like Adobe Photoshop. Colour inkjet printers can produce amazing results very cheaply these days and although there may be some question over how well the inks survive over time you can at least save the computer file and print it out again later!

Video

Editing is what makes a home movie good and even if the shooting isn't that amazing then editing can make the final product bearable. However, until the advent of digital video formats editing was an expensive and cumbersome business. Now it is possible to use computer software to edit sound and vision in a very intuitive way and produce a result which is, technically at least, excellent. If you or your friends don't have access to such equipment then see if you can find a local arts centre that does.

If you are a key participant in the ceremony then don't expect to be camera-person and director as well – although, of course, you can help with the planning before and the editing afterwards. The possibilities are infinite but here are some points to bear in mind:

- Always have a tripod available, handheld camcorders are wonderful things but they're so light that camera shake is inevitable. Hand holding is fine for vox-pop interviews; moving around a crowd etc, but a whole home movie made in this way is exhausting to watch.

- Think about lighting. If the event is inside then some artificial lighting may be required in order to keep the visual focus on the participants. If it's outside then where will the sunlight be? There is nothing more disappointing than the fondly-remembered happy smiling faces turning into silhouettes on the screen.

- The camera-person will definitely need to be taken

through the running order so that they don't miss any key moments and it may be as well to do this on site so that other issues (like lighting) can be worked out as well.

■ Sound is often more important than vision. A cardiod or shotgun microphone will pick up most sound from the direction in which it is pointed. You may be able to borrow a tie-clip radio microphone for the main speaker. If the ceremony is outside then don't forget to use a windgag. It may also be useful to have a continuous sound recording of the whole event available that you can draw on during editing. Mini-disk recorders are useful for this.

■ Do not miss any of the planned dramatic moments or the final production may lack continuity. Make the most of them by focussing on expectant faces before panning out to the action.

If you're planning to present the video to your child on their 21st birthday then the big question is what format to preserve it in. It's impossible to predict how the technology will evolve but it's probably safe to say that a digital format is more likely to be readable two decades later and an optical storage medium, such as CD-ROM, is likely to be longer lasting than a magnetic one.

Suggestions for
ARTEFACTS
AND COMMEMORATIVE OBJECTS

BABY ANNOUNCEMENT CARDS

mr William Frances · son of Barbara + Malcolm. BORN 17th march · 7·50 a·m

an original
card is a
fitting way
to announce
an original
child!

Baby announcement cards are a lovely
way to declare the arrival of a new person.

You could draw, cut out, print or paint the
cards yourself using imagery you feel is
suitable.

The cards could be like postcards, or sent
in an envelope. Think about what colours
you will use. Perhaps you could include a
photograph of the brand new child.

tom has been born to elizabeth fox 8lb 2oz · 9·11·98

It is also possible to design an original card and then take your design to the local printers. You can specify colour of ink, type and weight of card etc.

a birth announcement card from the Netherlands

A naming album is a special memento that can be created for and at the naming or welcoming ceremony of a child.

What is it? Essentially it is a book created for and about the child. The naming or welcome ceremony is a good opportunity to compile it.

What might go in it? Inside could be almost anything that fits the book format: photos, poems, drawings, messages, jokes, faxes, pressed flowers, cards, cartoons, cuttings ...

Who creates the album? The book itself could be handmade by a family member – it could be stitched, stuck, bound, folded from card, cloth, plywood or paper ...

It could be a beautiful book bought from a shop, or a plain sketch book that is decorated and embellished. It could even be a normal photo album or scrapbook. Whatever you choose ... the format can be big or small, square or tall. Obvious simple ways to make a difference are to re-cover it in wrapping paper or material, to cut the pages with a wiggly edge, to create a

great new cover with a photo and silver pens, or to interleave the pages with photocopies or coloured tissue.

At this stage the family or parent may wish to input the first contributions: baby photographs, something about the choice of name,

wishes. The next stage of creating is the contribution of friends and family at the ceremony. They may wish to just say hello, give words of advice, compose a new poem or do a drawing. You may wish to provide nice alternative pens for their use. It can be fun, though expensive, to have a Polaroid camera handy for instant snaps of the day to be added in. Don't forget glue for sticking. Think about where the book will be, perhaps an attractive table with a cloth. Think about when you would like it to happen. Don't forget to tell people there is an album and that they are invited to contribute to it.

An album can serve several functions:

- it is a means for family, friends and visitors to dedicate special wishes and words to the child for now and for their life to come,
- it provides a hands-on activity for the gathered individuals to feel involved in and part of the ceremony,
- it provides the opportunity to create an irreplaceable document that will always evoke and describe the unique occasion of this Naming Day.

The Life Book

I've always loved flowers, receiving them as gifts, picking my own. The colour and smell of flowers can really cheer you up which must be why we give flowers to people who are in hospital. Nowadays the flowers that you buy in the shops come from places like Kenya. It feels strange to think that they are growing them specially to export to the West so we can have any flower we want throughout the seasons. Fields that could be growing crops are growing Lilies and Tulips. I don't know enough about the economics behind it but it makes me feel that the bunches of flowers I receive are more than just a token offering. I started to press flowers because it seemed such a waste when they died. I didn't have a flowerpress, so I put them in a blank book and then under a heavy weight. It worked and I was enchanted by the way the petals became so delicate and faded. They seemed to mark the passage of time by becoming more beautiful rather than droopy, sad and smelly which is what happens to them in a vase. I started to label them with a date, or occasion e.g Daffodil to welcome me home. When I found out that an old friend of mine

had died aged 28 years old, the only thing I could think of doing was plucking a flower from the garden that was in full bloom and placing it between the white pages of the book. It wasn't only deaths that I was marking: my brother left London to start a new job. We went for a walk and he chose a leaf to press in the book to mark the beginning of a new journey away from all his family. We also started marking birthdays, finding seasonal flowers or leaves as part of a ritual that was often incorporated into a birthday breakfast or dinner. Many of my friends ask to look at the book to see how it's getting on, what additions I have made. It occurred to me that it was a life book because like a diary it contains extracts from life. The petals and leaves can't last forever but each time I look through the book I am reminded of people and moments that mean something to me. I've made a few life books for other people and they too have found it useful to mark occasions like births and deaths as a way of celebrating the miracle of life and coming to terms with the inevitability of death.

Tanya Peixoto

A time capsule for your child can be as simple as a collection of objects, thoughts or words gathered together at the time of birth to be re-opened later in life.

tin can time capsule

The time surrounding pregnancy, birth and early days is deeply significant and, for that child, will never be repeated. Thoughts, symbols, wishes and hopes emerge from heightened awareness. A time capsule is a means of capturing the potency of these emotions and "bottling" them. After much living has been done the child, or the adult, can revisit this personal and powerful box of treasures.

pop bottle time capsule

You can decide when is the best time to seal your time capsule. Perhaps you will gather objects for a year and then decide that you have a good picture of the child's first months. Alternatively you may wish to simply capture the days surrounding the birth.

What kind of things might go inside?

Things that have significance for you ...

Your baby's time capsule can also provide

ring box time capsule

a way to take a short cut back in history, so that the new adult may comprehend the times in which they were born. It's nice to recollect an era through tangible means.

shoe box time capsule

candle from 1st birthday cake

lock of Dad's hair before it went grey!

funny list of potential names that was drawn up

Your time capsule may also contain a special poem or gift to the future adult your child will become. The time capsule can travel with the individual as a simple symbol of their beginnings, or it may be added to throughout life as other significant occasions contribute to the richness of the treasures.

first vest that baby wore

photo of young parents

pressed flower from the garden

feather or pebble from a special walk on the beach

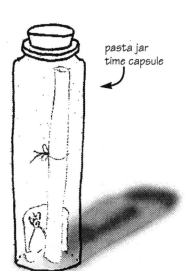

pasta jar time capsule

newspaper cutting

favourite CD of the moment

Growing Sticks are great sacred objects to accompany children through their growing years. They chart, in a fun and simple way, part of this unique child's development. The stick can become a personal totem charged with meaning and significance – for both parent and child alike.

Of course, in earlier generations – when many families lived in the same house for 20 or 30 years – the doorpost served as the growing stick. But with the mobility of the 21st century we need to find new and more flexible ways of maintaining this enjoyable domestic ritual.

Perhaps the best approach is to make one – a stick that is long enough and that you can take with you to your next home. It could be bamboo or dowel or a timber baton. You could paint it, nail it or stick things on. It could live anywhere – the kitchen, garden, the attic, your bedroom ...

you could choose a ready-made long, tall object ... a ladder is long but gives a strange 'achievement' image ...

a sweeping brush would do, but it's probably not the image you want either ...

you could scribe the height and date every birthday or more often

a spade has associations with growth and fertility ... but it's not very long!

Later in life, this slowly evolved three dimensional diary can evoke many memories.

ARTEFACTS THAT LINK ONWARDS

First Tooth

Links may be made later in life via an object or symbol, but it is also possible for the vessel established at a naming ceremony to be the lynch pin. Perhaps a time capsule was created for your baby at the naming. This seems the perfect vessel to contain your child's first tooth to come out ... put under the pillow first and then secretly added to the time capsule ... or added, with the child, ceremonially.

A link with later birthdays

If a naming album was created you may find it the ideal vessel to contain significant loose-leaf memorabilia that can surround future birthdays.

Photograps and letters have an ideal home in this album, as do birthday cards – cut up or selected from the usual abundance! Later additions to the album are the development of a wonderful visual and tangible diary of life events.

The Song of Life

We heard of an African tribe where – if a woman wants to have a baby – she sits under a tree until she hears the song of the child that wants to come. When she's heard it she teaches the song to the man who will be the child's father and when they make love they sing the song. When she is pregnant the mother teaches the song to the women of the village and they sing the song to welcome the baby. Later, if the child is hurt then people will sing the song to it, if it does well they sing the song. At ceremonies throughout her/his life the song is sung ... in fact right through until the person is lying on their death bed. Then the song is sung for the last time.

Ideas and drawings by Hannah Fox

How to make a
PAPER CUT

Papercuts are a simple and cheap way to make instant decorations or gifts that are both beautiful and bold.

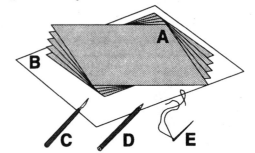

1 What you will need:

A several sheets of medium weight typing paper

B large piece of thick cardboard

C very sharp craft knife or scissors (preferably Chinese)

D pencil

E needle & thread or staple pliers

2
Invent your design. Beware of designs which include two lines crossing or "hollow" frames within frames. These will cause the papercut to become floppy or bits to fall out. Chunky kinds of images work much better. Trace the original drawing on to a sheet of typing paper and draw a frame around the outside. Quickly scribble over the bits that you are going to cut out.

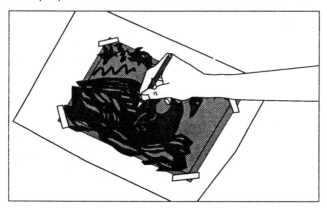

3 Now take as many sheets of typing paper as you require paper cuts and lightly stitch them together at the corners with the image on top. If you have access to staple pliers you may prefer to use them. You could also staple them to a board with a staple gun.

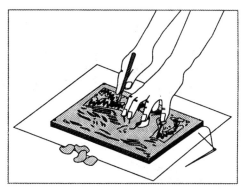

Disclaimer: Whilst all due care has been taken in the preparation of this information, neither the authors, nor Welfare State International, nor its members, officers, associates or employees can be held responsible for any omissions contained herein, nor for any damage or injury arising from any interpretation of its contents, howsoever caused.

4 Place the sheets on a piece of cardboard on a solid, flat surface and cut through all the layers at once in order to remove the scribbled over section. You may like to tape down the edges with masking tape. The paper cuts can be used singly or repetitively - perhaps taped over windows or unsympathetic fluorescent lights. **Do not use paper cuts near candles or electric lights that get hot!**

Design by Caroline Menis

How to make a
LANTERN

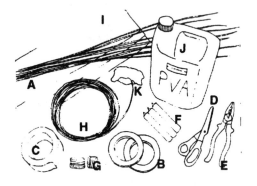

1 What you will need:

A withies (willow sticks)
B masking tape
C gaffer tape
D scissors
E pliers
F candles
G bottle tops
H thin wire
I strong tissue paper ("wet strength" tissue paper
J PVA glue
K piece of sponge/foam rubber

2 Cut four withies the same length for the base and join them at the corners with masking tape.

Disclaimer: Whilst all due care has been taken in the preparation of this information, neither the authors, nor Welfare State International, nor its members, officers, associates or employees can be held responsible for any omissions contained herein, nor for any damage or injury arising from any interpretation of its contents, howsoever caused.

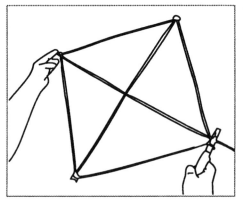

3 Add two diagonals. Measure the vertical withy to the height that you want and cut four of them. Join them at each corner and firmly together at the top. Decorate and strengthen the sides. Use a variety of designs - remember that they will show up in silhouette.

5 Make a door the same shape as one of your sections - either in the base or low down on one side. Fix it on with wire hinges. Make a simple wire hook to close the door.

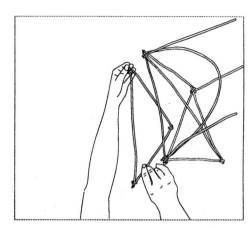

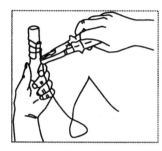

6 Use one piece of wire (approximately 1 metre long). First twist one end of the wire around the candle and loop it back on itself. Fix it into a bottle top. Bend the rest of the wire into four arms ...

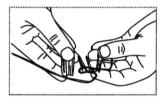

7 ... and attach them very firmly with gaffer tape to the base. There must be 12in (300mm) clear above the flame. **If the lantern is to be used indoors you should substitute a battery torch for the candle.**

8 Cover your table with plastic. Mix PVA with water (until it runs off the stick). Tear the tissue paper into manageable pieces. On the table spread the PVA over the whole piece of paper with the sponge.

9 Apply the wet tissue to the lantern, over-lapping each piece as you go. Cover the door separately so that it still opens.

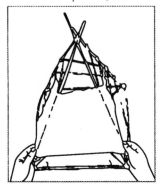

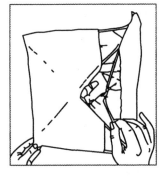

10 Cover the base and the sides, **leaving a gap at the top (above the flame) to let the heat out.** A final coating of PVA will strengthen the whole lantern. Add a wire loop above the candle, and you will need a pole with a hook (gaffer taped on) for carrying your lantern.
If you are using lanterns outdoors with candles and a lantern catches fire then try to ensure that it is away from inflammable materials (eg foliage and trees) and then allow it to burn out. You should not wear a shell suit or nylon anorak.

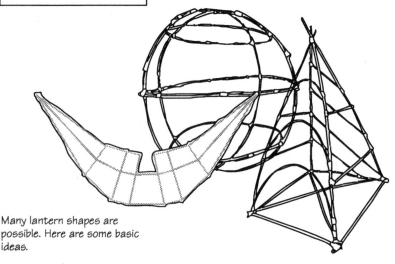

Many lantern shapes are possible. Here are some basic ideas.

CHECKLIST
A dozen things to think about when planning a naming ceremony

1 What do you want to achieve? What is it that you want the participants to know and to take away with them? How do you want them to feel?

2 You are likely to be able to fulfil your aims by the careful use of symbolism. Find ways to make links to earlier ceremonies (eg the parents' wedding); to family traditions; and to various cultural/spiritual strands.

3 Where will the event take place? Will the location make people want to come or will it seem inaccessible to many?

4 If the location will not be a place that you know well then make sure that you visit in advance. When you're there think particularly about vehicle parking, proximity of toilets and accessibility for elderly or disabled people.

5 The natural features of the location will often suggest ways in which a ceremonial space can be created. How can the symbolic and functional aspects of the design be combined in an elegant way?

6 What props or decoration might be required? Will anything need to be made specially? Remember to allow enough time. Will you need to borrow or hire a vehicle to get them there?

7 What time of year will the event be held? Certain weather conditions may attract some participants and put off others. The season may also prevent you from doing certain things (eg the summer isn't a good time to plant trees). Get the invitations out well in advance so that people have adequate warning.

8 How long will the formal ceremony last (15 minutes is plenty) and will it be placed within the context of a longer, perhaps more relaxed, get together? The overall framework for the ceremony needs careful planning and stage management. It is a good idea to have a printed order of ceremony for everyone who attends – attractively designed this can also make a good memento.

9 It is a very good idea for someone other than the parents to lead the event (ie act in the role of celebrant). Who will this be? It could be a friend or it could be someone who does this kind of work professionally – in which case expect to pay.

10 Writing a script in language which honours the occasion is a skilled job. If you hire a celebrant then they should be able to help you with this. The choice of poetry and music must also be made carefully and you'll need to think about the practicalities of performance.

11 Other people (older children, grandparents, godparents) will be thrilled to make contributions. If it involves speaking or performance on the day then make sure that they're adequately rehearsed and know their cue.

12 Mementos are important in making sure that the naming ceremony is not just an isolated event. Whether it's making a video or getting everyone to sign a book – make sure that you're adequately prepared in advance.

Music

One family we are working with in Summer 1999 in Barrow-in-Furness have chosen, for their son's naming: **A Whole New World** from *Aladdin* and **Circle of Life** from *The Lion King*. These will be played on a domestic cassette player in the function room of a local hotel.

Music has the power to contribute an atmosphere, add an emotional dimension to the gathering and bring its own colour. The choice is between live music or recorded. Is there anyone in the family or friends who plays an instrument? Flute, violin, banjo, guitar, saxophone and accordion are portable, go-anywhere instruments. Pianos are great but usually fixed indoors. Getting someone up who enjoys singing a song (solo or duet), can work well - and offer something unique and in the moment. Choose what makes you feel good – favourite songs, cultural references, geographical, seasonal ... Does the chosen name feature in a popular song? Hey, Jude?... Something funny or light-hearted, something from a nursery repertoire can be good when there are other children present. A piece of music can help gather and focus everyone at the start of your ceremony. Likewise, bringing everything to a close can be marked by a final piece of music. It's good for the celebrant to let people know what the music will be, and why it has been chosen. As it comes to a close, people feel comfortable to get up, move off, knowing that the focussed part of the ceremony is over.

Poetry

In addition to the poems scattered throughout this book you might consider some of the following: "A prayer for my daughter" by W B Yeats; "Frost at midnight" by Samuel Taylor Coleridge; "To my daughter" by Stephen Spender. In most cases an extract will suffice. The following books are good sources: **Generations: poems between Fathers, Mothers, Daughters, Sons**, edited by Melanie HART and James LOADER, Penguin, 1998. **Great Occasions – an anthology of prose and poetry** edited by Carl SEABURG, Skinner House. **A Time to be Born** by Jeni Couzyn, Firelizard, 1999 (available from PO Box 26327, London N8 8WU).

Books

Our Secret Names
Leslie Alan DUNKLING,
Sidgwick & Jackson,
London, 1981

Naming-Day in Eden
Noah JACOBS, Victor
Gallancz, London, 1958
**Baby Name Personality
Survey**
Bruce LANSKY and Barry
SINROD, Meadowbrook
Press, New York, 1990

**How, Then, Shall we
Live?**
Wayne MULLER, Bantam
Books, New York, 1996

New Arrivals
Jane WYNNE WILSON,
British Humanist
Association, London, 1999

**Engineers of the
Imagination – the WSI
handbook**
Baz KERSHAW and Tony
COULT, Methuen 1983,
revised 1990

The Continuum Concept
Jean LIEDLOFF, Arkana,
1989

**Circle of Life: rituals from
the human family album**
David COHEN (ed),
Aquarian Press, 1991

Addresses

**MUSICIANS' UNION -
Regional Offices**
North/North East Office
Tel: 0113 248 1335
North West Office
Tel: 0161 236 1764
Midlands Office
Tel: 0121 622 3870
East Office
Tel: 020 7582 5566
South East Office
Tel: 020 7582 5566
South West Office
Tel: 0117 926 5438
Scottish Office
Tel: 0141 248 3723
Welsh Office
Tel: 029 2046 1205

**REGIONAL ARTS
BOARDS**
Northern Arts Board
Tel: 0191 281 6334
North West Arts Board
Tel: 0161 834 6644
Yorks & Humberside Arts Brd
Tel: 01924 455555
West Midlands Arts Board
Tel: 0121 631 3121
East Midlands Arts Board
Tel: 01509 218292
Eastern Arts Board
Tel: 01223 215355
South East Arts Board
Tel: 01892 515210
Southern Arts Board
Tel: 01962 855099
South West Arts Board
Tel: 01392 218188

London Arts Board
Tel: 020 7240 1313

**British Humanist
Association**
47 Theobalds Road,
London WC1X 8SP
Tel: 020 7430 0908

Baby Naming Society
66 High Street
Pershore, Worcestershire
WR10 1DU
Tel: 01386 555599

**SANDS (Stillbirth and
Neonatal Death Society)**
28 Portland Place, London
W1N 4DE
Tel: 020 7436 5881

L A Mustgrove & Son
Lake Wall,
Weston Zoyland,
Bridgwater, Somerset
TA7 0LP
Tel: 01278 691759
Supplier of withies for
lantern making.

Web Sites

For an up-to-date page of links refer to the WSI web
site at:

http://www.welfare-state.org

Nanobaby
http://www.motivesoft.demon.co.uk/cyberzoo/nanobaby.htm
Take care of your nanobaby and give it a name!

Baby Names
http://www.babynames.com
Personalised service, name lists, "Baby pic-of-the-month".

Parent Zone
http://www.parentzone.com/parents/bnames.htm
Names along with meanings.

Jellinek's
http://www.jellinek.com/baby
Biggest directory on the Internet, voting system.

Dawn's Baby Name Software
http://www.dawnsoft.com/babyname.html
*11,000 rare and unique names. Your own search criteria:
meaning, gender, initial, final letter, uniqueness, length.*

Baby Zone
http://babyzone.com/babyname.htm
Name inventor, search database, logical names for twins!

British Humanist Association
http://www.humanism.org.uk/frcereremo.htm
Overview of the non-religious ceremonial work of BHA.

Loving Hearts Ceremonies
http://www.interfaith.org/light
Create personalised ceremonies for people of all faiths.

Society of Kabalarians
http://www.kabalarians.com
300,000 baby names, order your own name report.

American Name Society
http://www.wtsn.binghamton.edu/ANS
Promotes onomastics – study of names and naming practices.

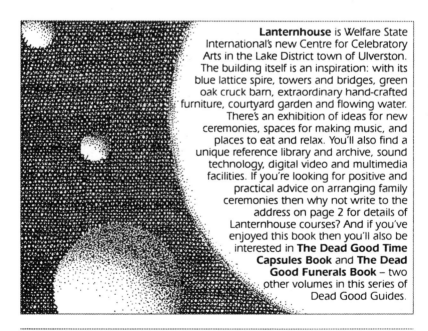

Lanternhouse is Welfare State International's new Centre for Celebratory Arts in the Lake District town of Ulverston. The building itself is an inspiration: with its blue lattice spire, towers and bridges, green oak cruck barn, extraordinary hand-crafted furniture, courtyard garden and flowing water. There's an exhibition of ideas for new ceremonies, spaces for making music, and places to eat and relax. You'll also find a unique reference library and archive, sound technology, digital video and multimedia facilities. If you're looking for positive and practical advice on arranging family ceremonies then why not write to the address on page 2 for details of Lanternhouse courses? And if you've enjoyed this book then you'll also be interested in **The Dead Good Time Capsules Book** and **The Dead Good Funerals Book** – two other volumes in this series of Dead Good Guides.

INDEX